Selena's Secret

THE REVEALING STORY BEHIND HER TRAGIC DEATH

Maria Celeste Arrarás

A FIRESIDE BOOK

PUBLISHED BY SIMON & SCHUSTER

For Manny

FIRESIDE
Rockefeller Center
1230 Avenue of the Americas
New York, NY 10020

FIRESIDE and colophon are registered trademarks of Simon &
Schuster, Inc.

PRODUCED BY K&N BOOKWORKS
DESIGNED BY RICHARD ORIOLO
TRANSLATED BY GUSTAVO MEDINA

Manufactured in the United States of America

10 9 8 7 6 5 4

Library of Congress Cataloging-in-Publication Data is available.

ISBN 0-684-83193-7

ACKNOWLEDGMENTS

For believing in this project and for all their help: Becky Cabaza, Gustavo Medina, Raúl Mateu, Dan Lane, Sue Fleming-Holland, Al Rojas and Fernándo López.

For their support and trust: Ray Rodríguez, Alina Falcón and María López.

For sharing their photographs: Emérito Pujol, Manny Hernández, Alex Franco, Ramón Hernández, Norma Jean Sierra, Doraliz Ramos and Fernando Diez.

For their expert advice: Jorge Rangel, J. C. Castillo, Gustavo Sánchez, Joe Bonilla, Irma Negroni and the members of the WW club.

For their help with the computer: Vivian Tous, Alfredo del Portillo and María Elena Figueredo.

For her prayers: Tata.

For their contribution to the Univisión coverage of the Saldívar trial: Ricardo Vela, Angel Matos, Ivan Rodríguez, Carlos García, Jorge Alvarez, Jerry Johnson, Steve Lipsey,

María Antonieta Collins, Neida Sandoval, Javier Colmeneros, Janneth Quintero, Malena Pedroso, Bert Delgado, Vivian Quevedo, Mari García Márquez, Cristina Londoño, Silvia Rosabal, Jonia Fernández, Javier Soto and Gisela Robles.

Special thanks to my coanchor Myrka Dellanos-Loynaz, who worked hard in Miami while I was in Houston for the trial.

CONTENTS

"Intimacy ends where secrets begin."

I confess that I wrote many of these pages with Selena's music playing in the background. I did it so that I would not lose my perspective and forget who she really was. Her voice and her songs will always keep me in touch with the human side of this tragedy. While I was writing this book, they kept me from going too far in one direction in my struggle to remain objective. After all, Selena is no longer here to speak for herself.

The music was also a shield. It protected me from Yolanda, who ended Selena's life. During our conversations, Yolanda could be charming and open, but the songs helped me to remember that it was she who silenced a beautiful voice.

I know Selena's secret.

—MARIA CELESTE ARRARAS, NOVEMBER 1996

1

March 31, 1995: A Star Has Died

"Selena's been shot!" someone yelled. I heard the announcement shortly after 2 P.M. on that Friday afternoon as I walked through a hallway at Univisión, on my way to the newsroom of the network's news division. That is where the offices of my show, *Primer Impacto,* are located. At first I mistakenly thought that the victim of the gunshot had been Selegna, a well-known Miami psychic who often appears on television. As incredible as this may sound now, my first thought was that the shooting was part of a conspiracy, an organized plan to finish off psychics and astrologers; two weeks earlier an astrologer who had a radio show had been shot to death in Miami, where our show is based. Perhaps the murderer was a serial killer unhappy with his astrological forecasts. New York City already had its own zodiac killer—a name assigned to him after he threatened to kill one person on the first day of each astrological cycle.

I flew into the newsroom on an adrenaline high and asked the producers to immediately contact Walter Mercado, the internationally famous astrologer who hosts the horoscope segment of our show, to get his reaction on what was happening. They all gave me puzzled looks, clearly wondering what I was talking about. But María López, the executive producer of *Primer Impacto,* had been watching me and seemed to know exactly what was going through my head without my having to explain myself. I think her brain and mine work alike. She told me that I had misunderstood what I had heard and made the victim's identity clear: "It's not Selegna. It's *Selena,* the queen of Tejano music ... and it's looking pretty serious."

As soon as María finished her words we all fell into deep silence. My colleagues had found out the news just a few moments before I had and had yet to catch their breath. Selena had been a guest on our show several times. Her last appearance had taken place barely three weeks earlier. This time the victim was not a name without a face. It was someone we knew. We all liked her because despite her fame, she never put on airs of being a superstar. On the contrary, she was quite down to earth.

Within seconds we swung into action. We had to immediately interrupt regular programming to report the event. At that moment our professional commitment had priority over any of our personal feelings.

A powerful charge filled the air and took hold of our group—that special current that flows through every journalist who realizes they've come across a truly major piece of news. That energy becomes our fuel, allowing us to work long hours with enthusiasm, without thought of food or sleep. That day we were going to need it.

Moved by that unusual force, we leaped to our tasks. Within fifteen seconds, I was seated at the Univisión news desk in front of the standing cameras. I did not have the time to run to the studio on the other side of the building where *Primer Impacto* is taped. With news like this, you cannot afford to waste one single second. As I hastily put on my mike and earpiece, arrangements were being made to interrupt our regular programming. The earpiece, which we call the IFB, is connected to a cable line that allows us to receive instructions from the producer and director who work from the control room. The technological magic of this little device has come to our rescue innumerable times like this one, when we receive late-breaking news and we are forced to improvise.

I remember turning around and seeing an army of people glued to their phones, frenetically hunting for any details of what was happening to Selena. The room was tense. We were working against the clock, trying to break the news before anyone else. The goal was to provide the greatest amount of information possible in that first bulletin. We knew Selena had been shot in a motel in Texas and had been taken to a hospital where she was undergoing emergency surgery. Other than that we had no clue.

Less than ten minutes after we'd learned of the shooting, I went on the air live to report what we had managed to verify up to that moment: "Good afternoon. I'm María Celeste Arrarás. We interrupt the program you are watching to inform you that Selena Quintanilla Pérez, the lead singer for Los Dinos, has been shot and is now in critical condition at Corpus Christi Memorial Medical Center. Right at this moment she's undergoing surgery. Selena was shot at the Days Inn motel of that city and details of the incident are still unknown. We are getting news bit by bit. As soon as we learn more about what happened at the motel and the singer's condition we will bring you an update."

We did it. We were first with the news. Normally, this is cause for celebration and congratulations. In the world of news reporting, timeliness and credibility are of utmost importance and are achieved only by being first on the air with the most precise account of an event. But this victory was a bittersweet one. The news could not have been sadder or touched us more deeply.

After the news brief I turned to my computer. There still was nothing to be found on the wire services about this event in Texas, which meant that we were way ahead of the other news media.

The phones at Univisión would not stop ringing. Viewers were calling in disbelief, hoping we would tell them we had made a mistake. At that moment, even we did not imagine that we were facing the most important news of the year for Hispanics.

Our news team had its hands full: searching for videos of Selena, calling the Days Inn, the hospital, the singer's home, her boutiques, her friends, her relatives. The information we were getting was contradictory and there were no reliable sources we could count on to keep our public informed.

Again I sat down at the Univisión news desk. Once more I hooked myself up to all the electronic tools that helped me stay in touch. I started writing down all the details that I knew about Selena's musical career. I wanted to be prepared in case of an important development, and thanks to that effort what happened next did not catch me off guard. After a couple of minutes, the show's associate producer told me, "There's bad news. We're on the line with the hospital and it looks like Selena's condition is worse." Alina Falcón, the vice president of the news department, gave orders to interrupt regular programming once again. Tragically, it was the right decision. At the very moment when I opened my mouth to report on the late-breaking developments, and just when I was about to say that Selena had been wounded, the news we had all feared reached my ears through the IFB: "She's dead."

These words left me chilled to the core, as though someone had drenched me in ice water. In those thousandths of a second, many thoughts and feelings raced through my mind, but the habits of my profession helped me to respond rapidly. Neither my expression nor my words betrayed me. I heard myself announce that Selena had died.

When the special bulletin was over I thought of how young Selena was. She was only twenty-three years old! What could possibly have happened? A wave of terrible rumors rocked us in the minutes that followed. Someone heard a conversation on the internal radio frequency used by the Corpus Christi police. One officer was saying that it was all due to a love triangle between Selena and the Tejano music singer Emilio Navaira, who was also married. Supposedly his wife had shot Selena after surprising the two in each other's arms. The rumor was reported on some local radio stations but was quickly dismissed. Then there was gossip that Selena's assistant had killed her in a confrontation that hinted at a lesbian affair. But we aired nothing of what we heard until we were able to ascertain what was true. We avoided the temptation of repeating unsubstantiated rumors just to make the news more impressive. For that reason, I feel proud that nothing was ever said on our show that did not adhere strictly to the truth. My team shares those journalistic ethics and although there are those who say that our show smacks of sensationalism, on that day we proved, once again and above all, that *Primer Impacto* is a responsible show.

In the middle of the afternoon I really felt the absence of my cohost, Myrka Dellanos-Loynaz. Of all days to have off! When there are two anchors and there is breaking news like this, the pressure is not as intense because it is being shared. Not only is the actual workload carried by two people, but also when you go live on the air it is much easier to squeeze out of a tight spot. As one of us is speaking, the other one is mentally rehearsing what she will say next or is listening to instructions via the IFB. When you are alone in front of the camera and have to improvise because there are last-minute changes or new information, you are forced to simultaneously concentrate on what you are saying and pay attention to whatever it is you are being told from the control booth. Believe me, there is an art to talking and listening at the same time and to being able to make what you are saying come across as logical and coherent. It takes years of training to learn this skill.

At one point, we received a call from the reporter we had sent to the Days Inn. She had verified that Selena had been shot by the woman who managed her clothing business. Her name was Yolanda Saldívar. But there was more: The suspect had holed up inside a pickup truck in the motel's parking lot. At that exact moment, she was holding a gun to her head, threatening to kill herself.

The show's producers flew into a frenzy. They were immediately trying to get a satellite feed from Corpus Christi to obtain live coverage from the Days Inn. In order to save time—we were in the midst of preparing for our 5:00 edition of *Primer Impacto*—we moved a TV camera to my desk in the newsroom, where I had my computer and the wire service updates at my fingertips. I would be able to continue working on my script for that evening's broadcast while at the same time updating viewers with special bulletins as I received information through the wires.

Just a few minutes before the start of *Primer Impacto,* I passed the control room on the way to the set. Madness reigned. There were so many reports coming in from the news wire at the same time that a river of paper was flowing from the printer. The telephones rang incessantly. The director shouted instructions nonstop. On the various TV monitors I could see half a dozen of our correspondents getting ready to go live during the show. They awaited their turns in front of Selena's boutique in Corpus Christi, in front of her store in San Antonio, at the hospital and in front of the singer's house. Our Los Angeles correspondent already had several people lined up, waiting for their reaction to the tragedy. María López talked into two phones at the same time, giving instructions to each of the *Primer Impacto* bureaus in Texas that she had on the line. She slammed down one receiver and continued the other conversation. "I want live coverage [of Yolanda Saldívar] *right now*!" she hollered, pounding the table with her fist. "We have to start with that!" In order to get the job done, an executive producer has to be strong-willed. Luckily for us, María could more than handle the job.

I rushed to our set with the script notes that I had made that afternoon in hand, knowing they might be useless. You cannot plan a show when the news takes on a life of its own. As I reached the *Primer Impacto* desk, I took a deep breath. I was ready for what awaited me. These moments of tension and uncertainty are the most powerful ones of our profession. For me, they are also a fascinating challenge. It was a great shame that all this energy stemmed from such a sad event. Unfortunately, that is not uncommon. News of this magnitude is often tragic.

At the top of the hour we began our broadcast. As the opening headlines rolled, María warned me that we were having an audio problem with the satellite signal from Corpus Christi. If we could not correct it in time, we would lead off with our correspondent in San Antonio. It was not what we wanted but we had no other choice. When I started my report on the afternoon's events, I received cues through the IFB to "stretch" my opening comments. The audio signal was about to be corrected. "Stretching" is TV slang for improvising, for killing time by talking; it allows the technical crew more time to fix the existing problem. Lucky for us, we needed only a few seconds. As soon as I heard the producer's magic words "We're rolling; let's go to the motel," I introduced our reporter at the scene. It was riveting to watch the action unfolding there. Dozens of police officers, armed to the teeth, surrounded a pickup truck. From far away, the cameras could barely make out the figure of the woman inside who had turned herself into her own hostage.

Police were keeping reporters and their crews from getting too close to the scene. Now I understand why: The negotiations to obtain Yolanda's surrender were going nowhere. Using a cellular phone installed in the truck, she kept in contact with the agents but her other hand kept the gun barrel pressed to her temple. On more than one occasion she requested that all TV cameras be removed from the area. Months later during the trial against her, it became clear how tense and dramatic the conversations between the suspect and the officers truly had been. But on this afternoon, no one imagined that Yolanda was disclosing powerful information from inside the truck and that her words were being recorded.

In Corpus Christi, we went live to another location where a press conference was being held by someone who was not well known at this point: Abraham Quintanilla, Selena's father. Beaten down by his pain, barely able to maintain his composure, he confirmed what we already knew and answered a few questions from reporters. He acknowledged that the prime suspect had been employed by his daughter and declared that for some time they had

had problems with her because she was stealing from them. At first glance it all seemed very simple. The truth would prove to be far more complicated.

From there we went live to several other locations in Texas and California, finding people already in tears over Selena. From the control room we used different satellite feeds to capture the mournful reactions from across the country. We spoke with a tearful member of the musical group the Barrio Boyzz, a Latin group with whom Selena had recently taped a music video. We found him in Puerto Rico. His quaking voice made it obvious that he had just found out the news.

In the middle of the buzz and frenzy a producer rushed into the control room with a video exclusive—one never seen before—for us to air. Someone in our affiliate station in Corpus Christi had unearthed it in their video library and sent it to us via satellite. The tape shows Selena and Yolanda on the day the singer opened one of her two clothing boutiques, Selena Etc., a few months before the murder. The images barely fill twelve seconds of airtime, but during those moments the two characters appear to be displaying a wide range of emotions. They stand alone in a corner, whispering in each other's ears. Selena appears to be sharing a secret with Yolanda. We see how at first Yolanda's reaction is serious, then surprised and finally amused. Seeing them like this, gossiping and laughing, it was obvious there was a great camaraderie between them. But what secret were they sharing? What were they talking about? We watched the video in slow motion and the effect was chilling. They seemed so inseparable, such close friends. And to think that just a few hours earlier one of them had put an end to the other's life. Who would have imagined it? Even now after all this time, when I watch those images I get goose bumps.

After we aired the brief video, the lesbian rumors increased. Those who did not know the protagonists of this drama reached their own dirty-minded conclusions merely because the shooting involved two women in a motel room. During a commercial break I heard one of the studio cameramen say suggestively, "Seems to me that something very strange happened there." This disturbed me. It wasn't just the comment by itself; it was the innuendo and the morbid joy in his tone. I sensed that another cameraman standing nearby had read my thoughts because he cut him off brusquely: "Hey, guy, give it a rest ... What a pervert!"

In short, we dedicated the entire program to the topic of Selena's death. Even our meteorologist, John Morales, who usually was caught up in his weather satellites and forecasts and who had yet to learn of the events, had to do a last-minute weather forecast for Corpus Christi. It would rain that night.

To close the show we repeated part of the interview we had done with Selena weeks earlier. Ironically, it had become the last live interview Selena would ever give. Watching her talk about her plans for the future gave the show an unforeseen dimension. It would chill anyone's blood. I remember her describing her dream home. She had bought ten acres of land in Corpus near some botanical gardens and described how in the early evening hundreds of birds would fly by. She wanted to build the house overlooking a lake because "it was the most romantic view of the property." Now this would never be.

Thankfully, the show came out "clean," without technical errors, as we say in our business. Our viewers would never know we had been walking on egg shells from beginning to end. And we had never looked down.

The standoff seemed endless. We were ready for a resolution at any moment. Since our national edition is not seen in California until three hours later, we stay at the studio whenever there are new developments in a major news story so we can air them live on the West Coast. In this case it was absolutely necessary. So we produced an entirely new edition for our West Coast audience. Yet when we finished at 9:00 P.M. Miami time, negotiations between Yolanda and the police were still in the works.

Although it was a Friday night, we immediately had to start preparing a special show dealing with the events for the following Tuesday's regular late-night edition of *Primer Impacto*. The first thing we did was to send our then host in charge of the entertainment segment of our show, Mauricio Zeilic, to Corpus Christi to cover the funeral and its related events. Mauricio is much happier when you give him plenty of time to get ready for a plane trip. He needs the time to prepare himself mentally against his panic-level fear of flying. But on this occasion, despite the short notice, he was able to manage his fears in light of the magnitude of what was happening. "What time's my flight?" he asked gently. In a few hours he was on board a jet like a true professional.

Without a moment's break, we contacted all our correspondents in Mexico and the United States so they'd be available to work the weekend. The storm of events required that we have the widest coverage possible.

As always, once we were finished with our broadcast, we were still wired. But once we were back to our relatively normal pace, I had time to process events. I could not rid my mind of the picture of Selena and Yolanda, talking privately and laughing like the best of friends. I kept asking myself the same questions over and over: Who was this mysterious woman and why had she shot such a sweet and charismatic girl? What had happened inside room 158 of the Days Inn motel? What was the one event that set off this tragedy? At that moment, I became determined to find the answers. I never expected that it would take me so many long months to find them.

Shortly after 10:30 P.M. that evening, I heard a yell as disturbing as the one that first told me Selena had been shot. "She's turned herself in!" I turned to the twenty monitors that cover our newsroom wall and I saw a whole gang of Yolandas, one on every screen. One policeman was covering her with a jacket to protect her from the cameras and the rain. John Morales had been right: It was pouring.

Although the officers moved Yolanda into the patrol car as fast as they could and sped her away, the seconds seemed to trickle by in slow motion.

It was at that moment that I had the instinctive feeling that this was not the end, but the beginning of the story.

CHAPTER

2

Special Coverage

"Selena? Her music is awful. I don't know what Mexicans are into. If you're going to sing about what's going on in Mexico, what can you say?... You can't grow crops, you got a cardboard house, your eleven-year-old daughter is a prostitute ... This is music to perform abortions to!" As these words were being broadcast on the radio—and adding insult to injury—Selena's music could be heard playing in the background interspersed with the sounds of gunshots.

The monster who made these pronouncements—just hours before Selena was buried on Monday, April 3—is none other than the radio talk show host Howard Stern. I cannot understand why he is popular among Anglo listeners, considering what idiotic things he says. But this time he'd crossed the line. He was rubbing salt deep into the wounds of the Hispanic community.

Stern had had problems in the past because of his penchant for insulting certain ethnic groups, women, gays and lesbians and others. But this time he wasn't going to get away with it. Though I am not Mexican (I am Puerto Rican), I lived in Los Angeles for a long time while I was bureau chief for the Univisión News division in that city. There, I learned to identify with them, to enjoy their sense of humor, to appreciate their culture. That's why I took Stern's insult as something even more personal.

In an editorial meeting for the show, I suggested that in order to support our people we carry out a crusade against this shameless man; that we join LULAC (League of United Latin American Citizens), a national organization that defends the rights of Hispanic Americans in the United States.

LULAC had broadcast messages to the Hispanic community to boycott the products of the sponsors of Stern's radio show. "We need to close ranks with LULAC and all the organizations that support the boycott," I said, indignant, and added, "We've got to put the pressure on so that we get respect and people realize that Hispanics, by their sheer number and purchasing power, are powerful." I was determined to support the boycott through my show.

I sensed that this cause would arouse strong emotions and I hit the nail on the head. Sofía Rodríguez, a Hispanic woman from Los Angeles, said on my show as we interviewed her on the street, "I wish I had him here in front of me so I could hit him." Francisco Cruz, another Hispanic from the same city, put it all very simply, "He is incredibly ignorant." When I heard people talking this way, I took the risk that afternoon of editorializing on the show. "His words should be repudiated. Even if he were to take them back, he could not undo the damage that has already been done. There's no excuse for this."

I called LULAC in order to get a list of advertisers whose products were to be boycotted if they didn't pull their ads off Stern's show. Unfortunately, they did not have available a list of national sponsors. LULAC had good intentions, but due to a lack of resources, its members were poorly organized.

The next morning, I listened carefully to Stern's show to find out precisely who his sponsors were. The show is heard all over the United States, but the advertisers change depending on the section of the country where the show is being broadcast. After it ended, I called Sears. They answered me with a strong letter: "Our corporate policy is that we are not associated with Howard Stern's show. We don't want Sears' name to be associated with his in any fashion. Selena had many admirers in our stores."

Next I called McDonald's. At that time I knew the company's public relations spokeswoman and I called her in Chicago. "How could a company with such a great reputation tarnish its image by advertising with Stern?" I asked her with a tone of reprimand. All my dear friend managed to say was that she could not explain how the ad wound up there. Later, McDonald's also sent me a letter explaining its position of disapproval toward Stern's show. Both letters were read on *Primer Impacto*. I also managed to broadcast the address and phone numbers of Stern's offices so that the public would overwhelm him with complaints. Shortly after that, a demonstration was held in front of the New York station from which he broadcasts his show. All signals indicated that the boycott was gaining strength.

In an attempt to placate the protesters, the radio show host sent out a video to the press in which he appeared apologizing in heavily accented Spanish. On the tape Stern said, "As you know, I'm a satirist ... my comments were not intended to cause more pain."

LULAC's representatives did not accept this explanation. Their national spokesperson came back with a strong reaction: "We want him off the air. We want to shut him up."

We broadcast his apology, but we made it clear it was unacceptable. Stern's attempts to pacify Hispanics after his unforgivable insults were "too little, too late," I said that day. Shortly afterward I found out that Univisión's president agreed with our decision to hit Stern hard.

The owners of a well-known chain of Texas supermarkets pulled from their shelves any products advertised on Stern's show. Unfortunately, except for this action and a few others, the effort had no major impact. At the moment our community was much more involved in mourning than in fighting.

During the days following the murder, thousands of persons flooded the streets of Corpus Christi and San Antonio. They carried lighted candles in their vigil. They prayed, cried and sang Selena's songs together. At the funeral something similar happened. On that gray day when even the sun would not shine, the condolences book was signed by seventy-five thousand people. The crowd was so large that at the last minute, the wake was moved from a local funeral home to Corpus Christi's convention center. The line to get in was so long that it wrapped around the building. Within hours, Selena's coffin was covered with more than eight thousand white roses, her favorite flower. Many of the mourners took a flower with them as a final memento.

Her loss was deeply felt. Perhaps what one of our Corpus Christi viewers, Estela Hernandez, said on our show is what best reflects what everyone was feeling: "You feel like you've lost part of yourself."

The news of her death found its way around the world. The *New York Times* put her on the front page and the BBC gave it extensive coverage.

The Los Angeles sport arena, the Colosseum, where Selena had been scheduled to sing on the weekend of her death, was transformed into a gigantic church where four thousand fans prayed for her during a mass. "The good ones are the first to go," said one of the assistants.

During the months immediately after her death about twelve hundred persons visited her grave in Corpus Christi every week; an equal number went to the Days Inn, which became a tourist attraction. The exterior walls of the room where Selena had been shot were covered with handwritten messages for her. One of them said, "Rest in peace, my queen." The public trooped through the room as though it were some macabre attraction. There was no longer any blood on the carpet, but one easily could see where it had spilled—the bleached-out sections made it obvious that someone had put great effort into cleaning it up. Eventually, the space became an ordinary motel room once more. But the number 158 was changed—in fact, all the rooms in that section of the motel were renumbered to discourage curiosity seekers. It's unlikely that motel management would have been able to rent out the room again had it not taken such measures.

In front of the singer's house her fans assembled a shrine in her honor. I could not help but notice a letter from a group of young brothers who were deaf. They had hung it on the fence. It said, "Selena, we were never able to hear your voice, but we could appreciate the beauty of your music just by watching you." From the window of a nearby house a tearful neighborhood boy observed the scene. Selena had invited the nine-year-old to lunch at McDonald's as a reward for having helped her rescue her lost dog. Her death had come just two days before their date.

In front of our eyes and our camera lenses a new cultural phenomenon was coming to life all over the country— Selenamania. People hungered for Selena. They all wanted to know more about her. And the more, the better. It was as though her death had left an emptiness that could only be filled with information. They needed facts about her life, about what had led to this tragedy and about the pain all Hispanics were suffering together. Responding to these needs, *Primer Impacto* produced a special show titled "Selena, A Star Is Dimmed," which we aired April 4, the day after her funeral.

For that show we traveled from coast to coast and found testimonials that were real treasures and that reveal the degree of Selena's impact on the public. In Florida, we found a Mexican lettuce farmer who told us that out in the fields he would always place a tape player on top of a nearby tractor to be able to listen to Selena's catchy beat. Remembering her, the old man cried like a baby. His sorrow went so deep and he seemed so fragile that I felt my eyes grow watery, and I had to pull myself together before introducing the next story.

We went to Chicago where her admirers launched hundreds of helium-filled balloons into the air. Each one was tied with a ribbon dangling a note that simply said, "Selena, we love you."

In El Paso, Texas, a huge star of lights that brightened the slope of one of the hills that surround the city was specially lit in her memory. All over the United States countless radio stations played her songs nonstop for hours.

We traveled to Monterrey, Mexico, where we found Gabriela Contreras, who could have passed as Selena's twin sister. Not only is she physically identical to her, but so are her gestures and her way of singing. A few months before March 31, she had contacted the singer but the two never got to meet. In Miami, we discovered little Leticia Rivera, who did get to meet Selena in person. Even at the young age of eight, she imitates Selena, hoping to follow in her footsteps when she grows up.

Both of them had dreamed of playing the role of Selena as a child and as an adult in the film about the singer's life, but this was not to be. Less than one year after the murder, during open casting calls in several U.S. cities, more than twenty-one thousand hopefuls showed up. It was unbelievable. Young women came from as far away as Mexico and Puerto Rico! Several newspapers ran the news on their front pages, with good reason. Only once before in Hollywood history had there been enthusiasm like this—during the auditions for the role of Scarlett O'Hara in the cinema classic *Gone With the Wind.* I remember that the headline on one newspaper in particular read: AN ARMY OF SELENAS. Underneath was a photo in which one could see an endless line of young women who appeared to be copies of the singer, carefully dressed and accessorized just like her. It was as though Selena were still alive and had been cloned thousands of times over.

Women imitated her; men worshipped her. On our special show we presented a man from Texas who went to the extreme of having Selena's face tattooed on his arm. Ernesto Gómez proudly showed us his colorful biceps. There is no doubt that the artist who did the work was a talented one—he was able to reproduce the face of the queen of Tejano music perfectly. The one person who was not at all pleased with this homage was Ernesto's wife. She, too, admired Selena, but she felt that everything has its limits. There is not one woman who enjoys living with her husband and "the other woman" in the middle. Over time she had no choice but to get used to it—the tattoo was permanent.

Our producers looked everywhere to keep our insatiable viewers satisfied. And they came up with some very interesting personalities, like the drag queen in San

Francisco who dressed up like Selena for a cabaret show. He did it with the hope of becoming a local celebrity. Ironically, like his idol, his life ended as his star was on the rise: He was hit by a car and killed. Even more tragic is the story of Gloria de la Cruz, a California woman who was known as Selena's double because of her amazing resemblance to the singer. She went to the casting sessions for the film about Selena and months later her body was found in a trash dump in Los Angeles. Her killer had strangled her and then set her body on fire.

We also found Juvenal Marín, a Californian who claimed to be a medium between the star and the earthly sphere. He insisted that Selena had come to him in a vision he'd had while meditating under a tree. She floated atop a cloud, telling him that she'd chosen him especially to deliver her message to her fans: She was at peace and they need not suffer any longer for her. Perhaps some viewers took comfort in his words, but most were probably amused.

Selena's face graced the covers of many magazines throughout the country and all over Latin America. *People* magazine did several major stories on her and those editions sold out so rapidly that more printings were ordered.

People later paid homage to the singer with a special edition totally dedicated to her—a tribute that had been paid before only to Jacqueline Kennedy Onassis, the former first lady of the United States, and Audrey Hepburn, the legendary Hollywood actress. More than 1.5 million copies of this edition were sold. (The magazine's publisher was so surprised and impressed by the sales figures that it has now launched a quarterly edition of *People* in Spanish.)

Selena was honored everywhere. The governor of Texas declared April 16, 1995 to be Selena Day. She would have celebrated her twenty-fourth birthday on that date and more than a thousand fans showed up at the cemetery carrying musical instruments to sing "Las Mañanitas," a Mexican birthday song, in front of her grave. The Houston City Council changed the name of Houston's Denver Harbor Park to Selena Quintanilla Pérez Park. In Washington, D.C., the Hispanic Caucus Institute of Congress honored the singer at its annual gala dinner. In Corpus Christi, the city that watched her grow up, the name of Bayfront Plaza Auditorium was changed. Now it would be known as Selena Auditorium. An effort was made in Corpus to change the name of a street to that of Selena's, but the noble gesture became a fiasco when it was learned that the street in question would have crossed perpendicularly to another street named Yolanda. It would not have been in good taste.

The singer also received smaller but meaningful tokens of recognition. In Santa Clara County, California, the week after her death seven out of every one hundred newborn baby girls were baptized with the singer's name. In the months that followed, at least six hundred baby girls born in Texas were baptized as Selena. In Houston, La Palapa restaurant created the Selena Special—two tacos, one enchilada, beans and rice.

The Coca-Cola Company, which had the singer under contract as a spokesperson, immortalized Selena with a commemorative bottle that bore her name. The limited edition of the soft drink sold like hotcakes. The profits were donated to the Selena Foundation, a new nonprofit foundation that awards scholarships to youngsters with limited financial resources and lends support to other entities that help children.

The Hard Rock Café chain put her name on one of their Hall of Fame stars. In its San Antonio branch, one can see one of Selena's favorite dresses—the beautiful white suit she wore in the music video for the song "No Me Queda Más." Months later when I visited the city for an exclusive interview with her father, I went by the restaurant and noticed that, like me, others came by just to admire her dress.

After her death, album sales broke records. *Amor Prohibido* sold more than 1.5 million copies. When her first and only recording in English, "Dreaming of You," was released a few months after her death, people stood in line at midnight in front of the stores. They all wanted to be the first to buy the CD. Within twenty-four hours, 75 percent of all available copies in the stores vanished, and in one week more than 300,000 CDs had been sold. Overnight Selena became the second female singer in U.S. history to sell so many records in such a short period of time. Janet Jackson is the only one to have surpassed her.

By the end of 1995, "Dreaming of You" went double platinum, selling more than two million copies.

Throughout the nation Selena's name was heard over and over. Those who had followed her before her death had even more reason to believe in her talent. For those who did not know her, especially in the Anglo population, a new, talented and tragically ephemeral voice was born. There is no question that one of the consequences of her death was to awaken the English-speaking public to the sounds of Tejano music.

How had she become a myth? What did people see in this unassuming girl of twenty-three years? What did they expect from her?

The border along Mexico and the United States has been home to immigrants from Mexico and their descendants for hundreds of years. Countless Mexicans leave behind their native land looking for their dream of prosperity and success. In their new homeland, these immigrants work hard and endure prejudice and economic hardships, but they do not give up. As the years go by they become the core of a new working or middle class. Not all their dreams may come true but the hope for a better life is passed on to their children. This is why when one of them or their descendants becomes a winner, when one of them crosses the frontiers of poverty or failure, they all win in some way.

When the girl from Molina, the classmate, neighbor and friend from that Corpus Christi barrio, started on the path to fame, everyone placed their bet on her with the wish that if her fantasy became reality, then someday theirs would, too. Selena, with her success and her songs, epitomized the hopes of the millions of Hispanics who pursue success.

Selena's triumphs were those of her community, just as her death was a cruel awakening from a dream that had just begun to come true. Even Hollywood opened its doors for her! Her brief appearance in the film *Don Juan DeMarco* could have been the beginning of a productive career in yet another medium. The evening of our special show we inter-viewed one of the director's assistants from the film. She explained to us that Selena had been chosen because of her great versatility, appearance, musical talent and charisma. "She could have had a promising career as an actress," she added. It was ironic that the picture had its premiere a week after her death.

Shortly before her tragic end she had also crossed the threshold into the world of television after her role in the hit Latino soap opera broadcast internationally on Univisión: *Dos Mujeres, un Camino,* with Erik Estrada.

People had been robbed of their idol, one of the lucky few who had made it. That is why they wanted to hold on to Selena forever in their memories and their music. This became obvious not only in the sales of her records but also in the frenzied way her admirers started to snap up any item that bore the singer's name. Her family started mass produc-tion of T-shirts, caps, coffee mugs, posters, jewelry, calendars and so forth. They also published a mail-order catalog through which one could order her designs for clothes and even Selena-brand jeans. It is ironic that before her death the queen of Tejano music had entered the world of fashion and had planned to sell her creations to the world. Those designs that were never actually produced appear in the catalog. The Quintanillas also launched four different fragrances for the perfume market, each one carrying the name of one of Selena's songs. One of the perfumes is called Amor Prohibido (Forbidden Love).

On the special edition of our show we also spoke with some of the motel employees. We did an exclusive interview with one of the maids who at the time was thought to be the only eyewitness to the crime. Rosario Garza gave her word but sullied it as well. She insisted on our show that she saw Yolanda shoot Selena in an act of betrayal right there in the motel hallway. "I heard the shot and saw how they both ran. I saw how Yolanda shot at her again. Then she went back into her room and later came out with something wrapped inside a towel and got into her pickup truck." Months later I was the first journalist to point out the serious discrepancies between this version of the story and the police reports.

Another maid, Norma Marie Martínez, also gave her version of the events on our show. For her, "Yolanda Saldívar was running after Selena and shot her. [Selena] started yelling, 'Help! Help!' Selena kept on running. Yolanda turned away as though nothing had happened." It is curious that she said nothing about what she later revealed in court, when she swore that she had heard Yolanda call Selena "bitch" as the singer ran in search of help.

There's no doubt that the show's most touching moment was when we interviewed Abraham Quintanilla. Our entertainment reporter, Mauricio Zeilic, visited him at his studios in Corpus Christi.

"My wife is destroyed," he began. "We're trying to find strength in our maker to keep going because we have faith that we will see Selena again on Resurrection Day."

Quintanilla declared himself to be astounded by the effect that his daughter's death had on the public. He seized the moment to thank people for the thousands of letters of condolence he had received from every corner of the hemisphere.

"Was Selena trusting enough to go see Yolanda Saldívar at the motel?" Mauricio asked.

"Selena trusted everyone," Quintanilla answered. "She did not grasp how popular she was becoming. She didn't believe there were evil people in the world. She liked to go alone to the malls and I would tell her to be careful. She would respond with 'Papa, please, you think everyone is a bad person.'"

He was intense about Yolanda Saldívar. "We had found evidence of fraud. We had a meeting—Selena, my daughter Suzette and myself—with her and she was not able to respond to any of the accusations we made against her. So we decided to fire her. Selena had her [Yolanda's] signature removed from the checking accounts and asked her to return some banking documents. She [Yolanda] used the pretext of returning the papers to lure her to the motel to kill her."

"Did you have the chance to talk with Selena in her final moments?" asked Mauricio.

"No, because when I got to the emergency room … she was already dead," said Quintanilla, his voice now cracking.

When he had just barely composed himself again, he lapsed into nostalgia, remembering his daughter's career. "It's so sad that she only got to record four songs in English!" As the interview concluded, he made a request: "My family would prefer that people not think of Selena as an idol—just a person who simply loved people," he said with a breaking voice.

Off camera, when the interview was over, Quintanilla shouted out, "Why didn't we get rid of [Yolanda] long ago! We knew she was an evil person!"

To conclude our special, we recounted the latest information regarding the events that had taken place just before and after the deadly shot:

Selena went to the motel accompanied by her husband on the night before the crime. He waited for her outside for ten minutes. In room 158, the women discussed a number of issues. Yolanda, who had just returned by car from Monterrey, turned over the documents Selena had requested and told the singer she had been raped in Mexico. But in her car Selena noticed that certain papers were missing. Shortly afterward, Yolanda began paging Selena on her beeper. Yolanda explained that she was bleeding a lot and asked to be taken to a doctor. Because it was late, Selena would take her in the morning.

The next day Selena took Yolanda to the hospital so she could be examined. The medical staff noticed that the patient presented clear symptoms of depression.

According to all accounts, Selena was the one who was speaking and giving instructions at the hospital and was constantly at Yolanda's side while her friend was being examined. Yolanda claimed that she had bled "a little" after the rape, upon which Selena replied indignantly that she had been told that she had bled copiously. At that moment everyone had the feeling that Yolanda was lying and that Selena did not believe her.

The nurse who attended to Yolanda was not able to perform the type of gynecological exam that would focus on gathering evidence of a rape; the medical center's rules would not allow an evidence-oriented procedure since Yolanda was a resident of San Antonio, the hospital was in

Corpus, and the alleged crime had taken place in another country. Had Yolanda wanted to make a police report, she would have had to do so in San Antonio or in Mexico.

The women left the hospital and returned to the motel. It was shortly before noon.

Inside room 158 the drama played itself out. At some point during their meeting, Yolanda took the revolver and fired a single bullet at Selena. The singer left the room running, bleeding to death. She got as far as the motel's reception area where she collapsed on the floor. The employees called 911 as they tried to help her. The ambulance arrived in no time.

Meanwhile, Yolanda, who had briefly stepped out into the hallway, reentered room 158. Shortly after that she left again, headed for the motel's parking lot and got into the pickup truck. When a policeman approached her, she panicked and aimed the revolver at her own head. In a matter of minutes several patrol cars showed up and she was surrounded by dozens of officers.

At this point we knew nothing more. Much later when I started to piece together the jigsaw puzzle of the revealing story behind Selena's death, I uncovered details that went deeper than the first simple explanation: Yolanda had killed the singer because she felt trapped after being accused of theft during the meeting with Quintanilla and his daughters. One of the pieces that did not fit the puzzle was that inside room 158 Selena had left a suitcase full of clothes and a permit to work in Mexico. Was the singer going somewhere? That suitcase had a peculiar destiny and undoubtedly played an important role on that fateful afternoon.

At Univisión, we were able to measure the intensity of Selenamania after we broadcast our special, "Selena, A Star Is Dimmed." The show received a rating of 30 points, which left no doubts that we were dealing with a major story. To give you an idea of what the rating system means, 1 rating point signifies that 72,100 households are watching a show. The show had drawn the second largest audience in the history of Spanish-language TV in the country. It beat all records and became a collector's video for those who loved Selena. We received so many thousands of calls that evening that the Univisión phone system shut down. Everyone wanted to know how they could purchase the video. The video was not for sale, but Univisión wanted to keep its viewers happy and aired the show again the following Sunday. The rating was 29 points. Almost as popular as the first time!

Facing the reality of the situation, Alina Falcón and Ray Rodriguez, the president of Univisión, decided to allocate all available resources—both technical and financial—to coverage of the upcoming trial. And thanks to the public's support we set sail on this adventure. When I was assigned to the project I felt honored. It was a major responsibility and I accepted it eagerly. From the very first day I had also felt drawn to the story and I wanted to get to the bottom of the events that had taken place inside room 158.

All summer our special coverage focused on the preparations for the trial. The state assigned Yolanda Saldívar a first-class defense lawyer, paid for by the people of Texas. He was none other than the veteran of legal battles Douglas Tinker, later named Outstanding Criminal Defense Lawyer of 1995 by the criminal justice section of the state bar of Texas.

Tinker is equally famous for his triumphs and his audacity. He loves difficult and complicated cases in which he can stand out. And many are the "almost lost causes" that he has saved. He is so confident of his abilities that at one time he even had T-shirts made up to give as gifts. The motto reads: IF TINKER CAN'T GET YOU OUT OF JAIL, YOU'RE PROBABLY GUILTY. In the past he had been the center of controversy when he defended a member of David Koresh's religious sect after the tragedy in Waco. But he had never had a client like Yolanda Saldívar. Everything and everyone was against her. At first even his wife was opposed to his representing Yolanda for fear that her family would suffer retribution from the community.

Tinker's opponent in this case was District Attorney Carlos Valdez, a Texas-born Hispanic. Like Selena, Valdez had grown up in the Corpus Christi barrio of Molina. A close friend of his told me that from the start, Valdez seemed to feel more than a professional commitment for seeing that justice was done; he was driven at a more personal level, because his family and the Quintanillas lived only blocks from each other. In addition, Valdez was facing an upcoming election and it was obvious that a victory in a publicity-laden case like this one would help him at the polls. His style was soft and elegant, his looks boyish despite the fact that he was in his early forties. He wore sober-looking clothes and professorial eyeglasses as if to compensate for his young appearance.

Valdez picked Mark Skurka as his principal legal counsel in the case. Skurka is a large man and a powerful presence in the courtroom. It is precisely because of his aggressive style, so different from that of his boss, that the two of them complement one another perfectly. Together they made a well-balanced team.

Tinker counted on assistance from Arnold García, a former district prosecutor with thirty years of experience. García, a Mexican-American who converses easily in English or Spanish, is a tireless investigator. Physically, the two are opposites. Tinker is quite tall and has such a thick white beard that one could easily picture him as Santa Claus. In fact, the resemblance is such that every Christmas he dresses up as St. Nick to give out presents to the poor children of Corpus Christi. García, on the other hand, is short and stocky, with an enormous black mustache. He has even jokingly compared his looks to Pancho Villa's.

The judge for the case was Mike Westergren, whom I nicknamed Judge Bow Tie. When he is not wearing his judge's robes, he can always be spotted in a natty bow tie. He is known for his discipline and control in the way he rules the courtroom and for his strong convictions. On one occasion he overturned a verdict after the jury found the defendant guilty. Westergren had recently been passed over for an appointment to Texas's Supreme Court. Still smarting from that disappoinment, he would have a chance to reassert his capabilities in the courtroom through the Saldívar case.

When the amount of Yolanda's bail bond was announced, the public responded with anger. A tearful viewer who called me shouted, "One hundred thousand dollars for bail is nothing!"

Lacking familiarity with Texas law, many people asked why the death penalty had not been requested for the accused. It so happens that in Texas the death penalty can only be asked for if a double felony has been committed. In other words, a crime has to be committed in conjunction with another crime of equal or greater seriousness. For example, if Yolanda had killed Selena while committing a theft, that would have been a double felony. Or if she had killed another person along with Selena, then the death penalty could have been requested.

From the very beginning I realized that the key to our coverage lay with two people: Selena Quintanilla Pérez and Yolanda Saldívar. Unfortunately, one of them was no longer with us. That is why, when I had barely started covering the news events, my goal became to speak with Yolanda. But how to reach her? I chose to be frank and direct. After much thought I sent her a handwritten letter in English, hoping to make it more personal. I did it in this fashion so her lawyers would be able to understand my proposal and assess it accordingly. In a thoughtful way, I introduced myself and proposed that, whenever she wished, we could have an interview. "I am the host of *Primer Impacto,* a program that is broadcast by Univisión throughout the United States and to fifteen countries in Latin America, including Mexico. Our program is the number one news magazine broadcast on Spanish-language television."

I then made my objectives clear: "I believe that fair coverage can not be complete unless both sides have had the chance to present their version. Therefore, I'd like to ask you for an interview in which you are accompanied by your attorney and where you have the opportunity to express your point of view. I give you my word that the interview will be done within a framework of seriousness, objectivity and respect."

I did not mention Selena at any point and I always spoke of "the events of March 31" when I was referring to the singer's death. Along with the letter, I sent her a photo of me to again make the communication more personal. Later I found out that of all the requests she had received, mine had been the only one to catch her attention. "It was the most humane one she received," her sister told me later.

My cohost on the show and I never referred to Saldívar as "the murderer." I was careful to choose terms like "the suspect" or "the accused." Like every defendant who goes before a judge and jury in this country, Yolanda was innocent until proven guilty. But in those days the sentiments of hate and prejudice against Yolanda were so powerful that many journalists stopped being objective.

I admit that I was careful in my characterization of Yolanda for other reasons. After sending her my letter I found out that Yolanda not only watched our show faithfully but that she also knew perfectly well who I was. I did not want her to think we were irresponsible. I wanted to lay the groundwork in order to earn her trust in a fair and professional way.

I also tried to reach her through her defense attorney. Bad idea. When I called him, Tinker was very curt with me. He told me that not at that point, nor in a month, nor during the trial would there be an interview with Yolanda Saldívar. "No way. Do you understand? And if it's up to me, there will never be one, so you're wasting your time." I remained livid and at a loss for words, but only for an instant. In situations like this one, one has to think fast or the opportunity is lost. I told him, "With all due respect, Mr. Tinker, I don't understand your attitude. At this very moment the entire world considers your client guilty. An interview can only help her case; she must have something to say in her defense."

In all truth it was not the best of arguments and I am sure I deserved what came next. Tinker interrupted me, "Miss, I don't owe you any explanations," and he slammed the phone down so hard I thought I would go deaf. I felt frustrated, furious, humiliated and ashamed. I knew I was only doing my job and that he, too, was doing his, but in any case it was a miserable experience. When the aftershock passed I became determined to obtain an exclusive interview with Yolanda. I was not about to give up the battle and I knew that with patience and perseverance everything was possible.

Much later my efforts would be rewarded. But what I did not imagine at that moment was that eventually I would make peace with Tinker and that he would wind up inviting me to lunch!

After Tinker hung up on me, I opted for another path. I called Arnold García, his defense partner. He calmly listened to my petition and never rejected the possibility that the interview with Yolanda could take place at some point in the future. From the beginning we got along well and stayed in touch throughout the process. Part of his job was to deal with the Hispanic media and, in particular, throw out "bait." Sometimes he would say, "You should take a look at a certain document." He would give no further explanations and I would follow his lead without further questions. Sometimes I would find details that were interesting and one of a kind; other times I realized that he was trying to throw me off the trail by giving me information that would take my focus off Yolanda. Arnold knew well the power of the media and its ability to change the public's opinion toward his client. But at no point did I allow myself to be manipulated and I refused to report on anything without proof or relevance.

One day I dialed the Saldívar family's phone number. The first call was the hardest. María Elida, one of Yolanda's sisters, answered. When I introduced myself I could sense the panic coming through the phone line. I begged her not to cut me off and she did not. In order to calm her and be able to open a door to dialogue, I told her, "I know Yolanda's lawyers have forbidden her to talk to the press, so don't tell me anything that might compromise you. Just hear me out." I told her about my intention to interview Yolanda but that perhaps this was not the appropriate moment. In the meantime I wanted to explore the possibility of doing a show where her family would speak. I asked her not to feel pressured but to discuss it with her relatives. I left it that I would call her the following week.

Even though the interview with the family did not become a reality immediately, I spoke with María Elida nearly every week in the months that followed. I thank her for having given me her trust and the gift of a lovely friendship. Little by little we moved from her one-word answers to comfortable conversations about her family, her sister in prison and daily life. That is how I discovered what a united, loving and giving family Yolanda had—and how much they were suffering. People treated them as lepers had been treated in biblical times simply because they were related to the person accused of killing Selena. They began to trust in me and to tell me about their Sunday evening prayer sessions when they would ask God to help Yolanda's cause. "When the truth comes out, everyone will think differently," they always told me. I was intrigued. Was there a hidden truth somewhere? To everyone the case appeared to be black and white. No one imagined that in reality it covered a wide range of grays.

During that summer I investigated every imaginable source about the lives of Yolanda and Selena. I read thousands of pages of all kinds of information. There was not one book or article that did not pass through my hands without notice. From each one I garnered some piece of information. Nor did any legal document escape me. Within the documents relating to various legal motions I found good leads that helped me obtain exclusive coverage. Everyone asked me how I did it. The irony of it all was that everything was right there in the court register. One only had to take the time to sniff around and search for it.

One afternoon I came upon various legal documents regarding Selena's estate. I decided to do a story for my show that would help dispel some rumors, in particular those generated by a Mexican magazine that had recently reported that Selena's father and her husband, Chris Pérez, were fighting over the money. Both of them were eager to speak to us at *Primer Impacto*—they wanted to set the record straight. And they didn't have to try too hard since it was obvious to our viewers that they were getting along just fine. The two interacted easily, like father and son. Abraham seemed protective of Chris; at one point, Chris patted his father-in-law affectionately on the back. Quintanilla made it clear he was extremely upset by the allegations made by the Mexican publication. He couldn't understand where they got their ideas from.

On the show, I explained in detail what had happened to Selena's inheritance. At the moment of her death, she was so young and full of life that it did not occur to her or to anyone else that her end was near. That's why the distribution of Selena's estate was done according to what Texas law stipulates when a person dies without a will. The heirs, her husband, Chris, and her parents, Abraham and Marcella Quintanilla, consulted the same lawyer as a group and together signed an amicable agreement to "honor the memory of Selena."

In terms of dollars and cents, the most surprising thing of all is that at the moment of her death, the singer and her husband had a total of $326,000 in joint assets: her boutiques in Corpus Christi and San Antonio, bank accounts, investments, furniture, clothing, jewelry, a motorcycle, her Porsche, a pickup truck and musical instruments. Because she and Chris shared this as community property, he inherited her half of these assets upon her death.

An interesting detail mentioned in the documents is that the heirs split among themselves what are known as Selena's intellectual properties. This abstract term means in plain language that the family will manage the businesses arising from any of the singer's creations. This agreement is private. Quintanilla made it clear in a later interview that the details were no one else's business but the family's.

The documents also grant Abraham Quintanilla the rights to manage all goods, companies and possessions Selena left behind. In other words, the singer's father became the executor. According to Quintanilla it is because he is the only one who understands the music business. Obviously Chris agreed. His domain is strictly music, not the business angle of music.

However, a legal expert we consulted believes that Chris made a mistake in not having a lawyer of his own to advise him individually. The expert and I discussed this issue on the show.

"According to the parties themselves, there's a close relationship among the family, the widower and Selena's father. Is this reason enough not to seek legal representation?" I asked.

"No. No matter how close they might be it's always recommended that one be represented by a lawyer. It's possible that Mr. Pérez may not have knowledge of the law, and if he does have it, it's quite limited. An attorney can always give him better guidance. It's possible that he doesn't understand the limits of the document he signed..." Of course, Quintanilla was not pleased when I revealed this information on *Primer Impacto*. It disturbed him immensely that I had consulted a legal expert and that on top of that the attorney "suggested" that Chris should have had his own legal representation.

Selena's assets seem paltry for a woman who was a musical superstar. *Hispanic Business* magazine had calculated that Selena had earned $5 million alone in the year prior to her death, which put her on the list of the twenty

Hispanic artists who grossed the highest incomes between 1993 and 1994.

So where is the real money? Everything she earned went to the corporation founded by the members of the Quintanilla family. Once expenses were covered, the profits were routinely divided among Selena, her father and her siblings. How this was done is not known with certainty but several sources have confirmed that everything was divided equally among the four. In other words, the singer was not a millionaire because she was receiving only a quarter of her earnings. Now that Selena is gone, Chris has taken her place as the fourth member of the corporation's board. It is ironic that even though she's dead, Selena's still a primary bread-winner for the family.

In any case, the estate, the properties or the money are but a small part of that rich universe which was Selena's life—no matter how short it was. Halfway through my investigations I discovered that Selena's life had much greater depth and complexity than what people thought. The same thing happened with Yolanda Saldívar. When I met her and found the opportunity to study her at close range, I found she was not as gray and monotonous an individual as everyone had thought. On the contrary, she is more like a complex rainbow, with the emphasis on the word "complex."

Without a doubt, for you to understand as I did what took place in room 158, it is necessary that you first get to know in depth the protagonists in this drama.

3

Selena

Selena got her name through a simple error in planning. April 16, 1971 was a joyful day for Abraham and Marcella Quintanilla. Their third child was about to be born and in their hearts they were convinced it would be a boy. They had everything ready for the new member of the family, whose name was to be Mark Anthony.

The woman who shared Marcella's hospital room, on the other hand, swore she would give birth to a girl whom she planned to call Selena. But fate dealt unexpected cards to both families. Instead of Mark Anthony, the Quintanillas had a beautiful baby girl while Marcella's roommate gave birth to a boy.

Neither Abraham nor Marcella had contemplated the possibility that they would have a girl. In fact, they were so sure they were going to have a son that they had not even considered a name for a daughter. The solution was simple. After talking it over, they borrowed the name that Marcella's roommate had chosen for her daughter. And so, Selena Quintanilla was born on Easter Sunday in Lake Jackson, a small town in southeast Texas.

The following day, Abraham returned to his job as shipping clerk and tow motor operator for Dow Chemical Company. His job was monotonous and, in all truth, it bored him. He had always aspired to much more: to achieving the artistic success that had eluded him as a young man.

His true vocation was music. During the sixties, Abraham lived in Corpus Christi and was a member of the group Los Dinos. In addition to singing, he was in charge of negotiating performance contracts for the group. The band had a certain amount of regional success and one of their songs became popular throughout the Southwest, including Arizona and California. But the never-ending road trips proved to be too much for Quintanilla, who by now had a wife and children. So eventually he had to leave Los Dinos and take the job with Dow Chemical. Five years later, in 1974, the group disbanded.

Abraham's frustration continued to mount as the years went by and he made a vow to reclaim his vocation—either on his own or through his children. Years later he would say to me, "When I realized my daughter could sing, I immediately saw the rebirth of my dream."

As a child, Selena was very active and athletic. She would just as easily play ball with the boys as dolls with the girls. Her sister, Suzette, recalls how even as a little girl Selena loved fashion and that she once designed an outfit in a bright violet color for one of her dolls. But her true talent was her singing, which was discovered almost accidentally. One day, her brother, A.B., was given a bass guitar as a present. Her childish envy drove the youngster to compete in any way she could. She picked up an old songbook belonging to her father and as he arrived home from work, she greeted him by singing the words to a melody she made up as she went along. Her voice and intonation surprised Abraham, who had always had a good ear for music. Yes, the rebirth of Abraham's dream had indeed begun.

In the early 1980s, the Quintanilla family took a decisive step. Abraham opened his own business, a Mexican restaurant that he named Papagallo's. He was so convinced that he would do well in this new venture that shortly thereafter, he left his job at Dow to dedicate himself full time to managing the restaurant. He had a small dance floor put in as well as a stage where local bands could perform. Naturally, the house band would be made up of his own children, who, under his direction, had put together a musical group they christened Los Dinos. This was not a sentimental gesture. Abraham knew that with a well-known name, the group would get more attention. Full of enthusiasm, Quintanilla covered the garage walls at home with carpeting and turned the space into a soundproof studio so that his children could rehearse—A.B. would play bass, Suzette the drums and Selena would be the vocalist. The stage lights for the shows were made by Abraham himself, using lightbulbs housed in empty tin cans.

When they made their debut at Papagallo's, Selena was nine years old. In an old video you can see the little girl, holding a microphone much bigger than her hand, singing "La Bamba." Her girlish body was deceiving since the voice that poured forth was as powerful as a grown woman's. You had to see it to believe it! Her father would glow with pride as he watched the audience's look of disbelief when they heard the intense voice coming from his small daughter. As he recalled those days, Abraham said, "Selena had the perfect pitch, the perfect timing. Some people go to school to learn music and they never learn it. These kids, within a month's time, they were playing four songs. They were gifted."

But luck was not with them this time. Papagallo's business went down when the oil crisis hit Texas hard and eventually fell into bankruptcy. The Quintanillas had to sell their house and they were left practically on the street. It was a very difficult period. Abraham changed jobs often and the family had to move numerous times. Finally, tired of living like a gypsy, he decided to return to Corpus Christi, where he had his roots and his relatives and where a new future awaited him.

In Corpus, Abraham had to start from scratch. Without capital or a fixed income and lacking a profession, he took on whatever was offered to him. He began by helping one of his brothers who had a truck rental business. But he was clear on one point—the job would be temporary. His goal was to get back to the music business, the world he knew best, and he was convinced he had the instinct and the vision to succeed in it. Besides, he knew he would never be content as someone else's employee.

He had the most minimal of financial resources to accomplish his return to music, but he could depend on his three children. Thanks to the lessons in the garage, the Quintanillas had learned the principles of playing instruments and singing. Since their first language was English, the youngsters learned songs in Spanish phonetically. Then, thanks to their father's coaching, they learned how to add the proper stress at the right moments to create the drama that made the songs come alive. Los Dinos were a family enterprise, with each member contributing in any way they could. The children made the music; Abraham ruled as manager and worked as sound engineer; Marcella took care of meals, giving everyone the support they needed, even learning how to work the lights during a performance. They bought and refurbished an old bus that they called Big Bertha in which they all traveled—even bringing along their dog.

During this period, Quintanilla would take the family out for drives through the priciest residential sections of Corpus. As he pointed out the mansions, he once told his children, "One day you're going to have it all. Don't give up." Little did he know how prophetic his words would be, though it would take some time before they became reality.

The first years were difficult. Los Dinos toured the state of Texas in Big Bertha—where they ate and often slept. They literally sang for their supper since the family had no other source of income. There was barely enough money for gas. Doors did not open easily to a musical group whose members were so young, with a lead singer who was but a little girl and, on top of that, a female. They were able, though, to change Selena's childish appearance to make her look somewhat older by using makeup and the right clothes. The transformation of the tiny singer would take place in a small room with a makeup table inside Big Bertha.

Curiously enough, years later, when Big Bertha was on its last legs, Abraham sold it to an events producer in New York. At the time the vehicle was basically junk on wheels and Abraham thought he had made the deal of a lifetime. But after Selena's death the man who had bought Big Bertha wrote me at Univisión to see if I was interested in his new project: He was going to fix up the old bus and turn it into a museum on wheels. He was thinking of painting it black, Selena's favorite color, and taking it on tour all around the country. It never occurred to Abraham that the old wreck of a bus would one day be someone else's treasure.

Between 1981 and 1983, Los Dinos traveled frequently and performed as often as they could. They did parties, weddings and birthdays; they played nightclubs and bars where the oil workers looked forward to their weekend shows.

While Los Dinos gathered momentum, Selena enrolled at West Oso Junior High School to continue her education. All her teachers remember her as engaging and intelligent. Lupe García, her American history teacher, tells the story of how one day in 1983 Selena announced she had recorded her first record and asked if the teacher would like to have one. García said yes, but when Selena proudly presented the recording, instead of thanking García for being interested in her music, Selena said, "That'll be five dollars." As she put the money away, she smiled and said, "These are the first five dollars I've earned with this."

Selena's seventh-grade teacher, Marilyn Greer, was not at all pleased about the child's musical career. For her, Selena was a talented and intelligent student with great possibilities, but Greer believed she was being used and her talents squandered, singing in bars on the weekends until 2 A.M. instead of living the kind of life of a normal girl her age. But the most serious problem was that her performance at school was going downhill. There were many Fridays and Mondays when Selena did not show up at school. During the week she looked tired. It is not by accident that Suzette Quintanilla recalls that during that period it was common for her sister to fall asleep during the breaks between sets.

Marilyn Greer discussed the delicate situation with Abraham and found herself up against a wall. He did not think he was exploiting his daughter and accused the teacher of not minding her own business. She threatened to report him to the Texas Board of Education. Eventually, Abraham took Selena out of school and enrolled her in a well-known correspondence course based in Chicago to continue her education. It was the same institute that had also provided courses for the world-renowned Osmond family. Abraham never thought he would ever again cross paths with Greer. Much less did he imagine that when he encountered her again, a decade later, she would be a key court witness testifying in defense of the woman accused of killing his daughter.

Selena's departure from school took place at the same time she took her first steps upward in the world of music.

After two years of touring all over Texas, Los Dinos debuted on television in 1983 to promote their new record on the *Johnny Canales Show.* The show was popular all over south Texas and had some national visibility as well. It was a major opportunity for Selena and Los Dinos. Thanks to the reach of television, they garnered legions of new fans and were on their way to becoming one of the most popular groups in Tejano music.

Selena's ascending career corresponded to the increasing popularity of Tejano music in the mideighties. The U.S. Hispanic population had swelled so that this "minority" consisted of nearly thirty million people at that point in time—a potential music market without precedent. In addition, there were the millions of Mexicans on the other side of the border, already fans of Tejano culture. It's not surprising that profits generated by Tejano music record sales grew at an amazing rate throughout the eighties and into the nineties. By 1994 the industry was generating sales of $50 million. Selena was in the right place at the right time—and she would prove to have the talent that would take this growing audience by storm.

It seems as though Selena went from a girl to a grown woman overnight. She began to wear clothes designed to emphasize her curvaceous figure. But she never came across as cheap—simply sexy. She instinctively seemed to know how to best use makeup and accessories without looking painted up or vulgar. She started watching her diet to keep herself looking svelte, and although she never had a weight problem, her body tended to be full-figured. This would obsess her to no end. She drank gallons of water with lemon juice and she herself would massage her thighs in a circular pattern, believing this would help her combat cellulite. She also saw herself as having a more than abundant derriere, not realizing that her voluptuousness was one of the characteristics her fans most adored about her.

Selena's coquettish and fun-loving stage manner also won her admirers. What few people knew was that this was not an act. Selena was playful—onstage and off. The Quintanilla family shared several of Selena's practical jokes with *People* magazine. Once, after her performance with the Tejano group La Mafia, Selena prepared a plate of Oreo cookies, secretly removing the cream filling and replacing it with toothpaste. Abraham happened to grab a doctored cookie before the musicians and took a great big bite. She looked at her father, frightened. But much to her surprise, Abraham did not notice anything unusual. In fact, as he chewed he announced, "These cookies are delicious ... they're mint flavored!" Selena erupted with laughter. On another occasion, while performing a duet with another singer, she jokingly stuck the shell of a sunflower seed in her mouth to cover one of her teeth, transforming her flawless smile into a comical grin. The audience did not catch it but her singing partner, who stood close to her, lost all concentration. Suzette recalls that afterward they could barely stop laughing.

Selena's clowning antics seemed to ease the stress of this intense period of work and travel. Other musicians who later joined Los Dinos recalled that during road trips, Selena would promenade up and down the aisle of the tour bus, microphone in hand, mockingly singing opera pieces.

During a softball game to raise funds for charity, Los Dinos beat an opposing team of deejays. The winners got to plaster the losers with pies, with Selena throwing more pies than anyone. Her joyfulness was contagious and her fans seemed to be swept up by it during her shows.

In 1987, she received the Tejano Music Award for female entertainer of the year. This honor, which she would go on to win eight years in a row, signaled a new, more serious level of success for Selena, though that first victory was perhaps the most unforgettable. Those who applauded her that night when she accepted the prize never dreamed that this young woman of sixteen would eventually put Tejano music on the map. And no one could have imagined that nine years later, in 1996, they would return to the same event to pay her a posthumous homage.

Two years after receiving that first award, Selena stumbled upon a great opportunity totally by chance. In 1989, José Behar, president of EMI Latin Records, was in San Antonio on a business trip. Selena was also in San Antonio performing at a nightclub. Behar happened to be passing by the club when he saw a crowd surround the singer after a show. The fans' high spirits caught his attention. When he was able to get close to her, he introduced himself as president of EMI Latin. Selena laughed and said, "Yes, of course." José Behar produced his business card and within minutes Abraham Quintanilla was making plans with Behar for a breakfast meeting the following morning.

Shortly afterward, Abraham's company, Q Productions, signed a contract with EMI Latin to produce recordings in Spanish. Eventually, EMI would release five successful Selena y Los Dinos CDs that would generate $4 million in sales in five years.

It was also in 1989 that Selena's brother, A.B., heard the music of Chris Pérez for the first time. Chris was a young, long-haired guitar player with a San Antonio band. A.B. was so impressed with his talent that he made him an offer on the spot to join Los Dinos. Chris left his old band and accepted the offer, not dreaming that this would be the most eventful decision of his life.

Selena was intrigued upon meeting Chris. He was quite reserved, but his manner was so warm and tender that the singer must have known he was capable of deep emotion. She also found him attractive and liked the stylish way Chris gathered his long hair into a ponytail. But for two years her curiosity went no further.

As time passed, the two developed an easy friendship. They spent lots of time together traveling, rehearsing and performing with Los Dinos, working hard—and relaxing when they could. Selena was totally dedicated to her profession and had grown up constantly surrounded by her family and various bandmates. It's unlikely she had had many opportunities to establish a steady relationship with a young man, and so perhaps it was inevitable that she eventually took a more serious look at Chris. Selena started to view him more as a man than as another band member and she confided her romantic feelings to her brother. A.B. was happy that his younger sister was attracted to Chris, now one of his best friends, and he threw himself into the role of Cupid. A.B. told Chris that his sister was interested in him and he mischievously asked Chris what he thought of

Selena. The guitar player was caught off guard. He thought of Selena as a good friend. He admired Selena's bubbly personality and even compared her passionate temperament to a volcano. But he had never dared to look at the singer as a woman. Until now.

After the conversation with A.B., Chris, too, began to see Selena in a different way, but he did not have the courage to approach her in a romantic manner. Chris was reluctant to express his true feelings. What if they were to attempt a romantic relationship and it failed? What if one of them were left hurt or disillusioned? How would they be affected professionally?

Selena seemed to have no such qualms and was not about to give up. She loved challenges. She also detected that Chris's shyness was a cover for his growing feelings toward her. She decided to take action. One afternoon when the two were having lunch at a pizza parlor, the volcano erupted. Selena confided in Chris everything she felt about him and asked him to allow her to get to know him better. Chris froze into an iceberg, although he was melting inside. He did not say a word. Finally, as they walked out the door, he gathered his courage and revealed his feelings to Selena. It was the first time he had opened his heart to a woman and he could not have chosen a more receptive one.

By the middle of 1991 the relationship between Selena and Chris was in full bloom. At first, many observers could not understand how such opposite personalities could attract. Selena was all woman, outgoing and never without a laugh. Chris was boyish and quiet with a shy smile. But it was obvious to everyone around them that despite their differences, the two were deeply and genuinely in love.

Abraham Quintanilla was opposed to the romance. He believed that the relationship and likely marriage would harm his daughter's career, stealing away time and effort at a moment that was critical both artistically and financially. He had always been very strict with his youngest and it was no doubt difficult for him to accept that his Selena was no longer a little girl. But surely he must have realized that one day this moment would come. Selena was bound to have a man in her life and Chris, at least, was a member of Los Dinos.

Therefore the distraction of a relationship would probably not amount to much. Despite Abraham's initial reservations, the hardheaded Selena got her way and she married Chris on April 2, 1992. The newlyweds moved into a house next door to the Quintanillas in their old Corpus Christi neighborhood of Molina.

Perhaps the most important year of Selena's career was 1993. The singer recorded a live album, *Selena Live,* a blockbuster success that went double platinum, selling more than two million copies. But even more significant, *Selena Live* was nominated for a Grammy for Best Mexican American Album. Selena did not expect to win, but was very excited by the festivities and felt honored by the nomination. As a twenty-two-year-old, she was competing for one of the most important prizes in the world of music! On top of that she was going to meet legends from the world of music and would have her photo taken with her favorite stars. Selena brought along her camera when she went to New York for the Grammy Awards. Ironically, she was not allowed to bring her camera in but, to her surprise, she left the awards with the unexpected prize in her hands. On *Primer Impacto* we showed video of Selena clutching her award as she left the Grammys. We were all happy for her.

The Grammy confirmed the upward direction her career was taking. Her increasing success at the regional and now national levels paved the way for new opportunities. José Behar had the idea of "cross-pollinating" two different musical markets in order to launch artists who had triumphed in one region but who had yet to be known in another. He would attempt this crossover strategy with Selena and the Barrio Boyzz. Although the Barrio Boyzz had found their audience among Hispanics on the East Coast, they had not been able to break into the Southwestern market where Selena reigned. But the queen of Tejano was unknown in the Barrio Boyzz's territory. Behar brought them together in New York to tape the music video for the song "Donde Quiera Que Estés." It was a clever idea that achieved the audience expansion Behar was after.

Taking advantage of these newly discovered markets, Selena and EMI released a new CD, *Amor Prohibido,* which, according to the critics, is the singer's best work. The album quickly became number one on Billboard's Latin 50 chart and the title track stayed on the top of the magazine's Hot Latin Tracks chart for two months.

The song "Amor Prohibido," inspired by a true story, was written at Selena's request, something which was not unusual. The singer would have a song idea and share it with A.B., who would go to work. As a songwriter, A.B. was the true talent of the family. And once he did his job, all Selena had to do was sing his song with her amazing voice. Selena and A.B. were an incredible team, working together to create their best-known hits.

"Amor Prohibido" is based on the story of Selena's grandparents, who, despite their class differences, fell in love and got married—defying society as well as family. "Como la Flor" was inspired by the illuminated flower decorations that are used to decorate dance halls. "La Carcacha" is a lighthearted tune based on a date A.B. once had; it seems the young lady was only interested in going out with him so that she could ride in his sportscar. "Bidi Bidi Bom Bom," one of her greatest hits and one that was especially liked by children, came out of some improvising Selena did during a rehearsal. During a break, the band started to pick out a song that had a *cumbia* beat, which then changed to reggae. Selena started singing, making up lyrics as ideas came to her. "Bidi Bidi Bom Bom" is about a young girl's unrequited love for a boy, and the title refers to the sound of her heart pounding as she sees him walk by.

In 1994, Selena had achieved celebrity status within the world of music and she seemed fulfilled as an artist. The prizes verified her standing as a major star and the concert offers were pouring in. She had taken her first step in Hollywood, appearing in the film *Don Juan DeMarco*. She had promotional contracts with major companies like Coca-Cola and her album sales seemed unstoppable. In addition, Selena was about to release an English-language CD—a defining step in her career that would guarantee her crossover success.

Perhaps because of all this, she decided it was the right time to bring her most precious dream to life: to enter the world of fashion. She had always wanted to become a famous designer; since childhood she had been passionate about clothes. And so, she founded a company that she called Selena Etc. and opened two clothing boutiques with beauty salons in San Antonio and Corpus Christi.

The singer had so many music-related commitments that she hired a young Hispanic designer, Martín Gómez, to create and oversee the production of the garments. But her long-range plans were to design the clothes herself and mass produce them. The boutiques were the first step in that direction. "Music is my career and fashion is my life," she once said. Ironically, it was not until after her death that Selena's family realized how important this goal had been for Selena. Up until then they had seen her interest in designing clothes as a whim, a pastime with which she amused herself. Suzette even recalls how they all jokingly teased the singer, telling her that she had opened the boutiques and beauty salons in order to pamper herself.

The Quintanillas' financial empire extended into many diverse areas in 1995. Just as Selena had started her own fashion business, her siblings and father also had enterprises of their own, though they were all music related. Abraham ran his company, Q Productions; A.B. focused on producing and songwriting; Suzette was involved in marketing. The Quintanillas found themselves consumed by what had once started out as a simple family endeavor. In addition, more and more letters from adoring fans were arriving every day, and they had no means to respond. A fan club must have seemed like the perfect solution for handling an important side of the business that none of the Quintanillas had time for.

The club started taking shape in mid-1991, when Abraham claims to have received approximately fifteen messages from the same person on his answering machine. When he returned the calls, the person proposed to him the creation of the Selena Fan Club, with the objective of promoting the star's career through tapping into her popularity among the growing legions of Selena CD buyers and concertgoers (she would draw more than sixty thousand fans to Houston's Astrodome, an attendance record for a Tejano concert event). Furthermore, the club would do charitable works to help the handicapped. Abraham mulled the idea over and agreed that it was a good one. Besides, this was help from the outside; creating a fan club would have taken away valuable time from his increasingly busy family.

The persistent caller would become the club's first president. Abraham could not help but take notice of her name—Yolanda—just like one of his sisters. Yolanda Saldívar.

4

Yolanda Saldívar

She was always the baby of the family. Yolanda, now seen as a monster by many people, had been considered the special one in her family ever since she was a little girl. Her father, Francisco Saldívar, is one of thousands of Mexican Americans who have inherited the shared cultures that surround the border between the United States and Mexico.

He and his wife, Juana, had eight children. They have always worked very hard: Frank has been a waiter at the same Mexican restaurant for over forty years and Juana has dedicated herself to making a home, taking care of the children and making snacks that are sold on the street.

The Saldívar family always was and continues to be very close. I met them at their most difficult moment, when the whole world was villifying their youngest daughter, though I never saw them act bitter, resentful or vengeful. If anything, they seemed sad. But they always had a smile for Yolanda, even when sorrow was gnawing away at them.

I could not have a better impression of the Saldívar marriage. They are a hardworking, honest and decent couple. They are Catholic and quite devout. They have done everything in their power to secure a solid future for their family, obtaining the best schooling possible for their children and instilling them with strong, basic values. It hurt them terribly that from the very beginning everyone passed judgment on Yolanda. They never considered their daughter to be a rotten apple. On the contrary, they believe in her and give her their support, viewing her as a victim of circumstance—a victim of what they believe to be the wickedness of Abraham Quintanilla.

Yolanda was born on September 19, 1960, in San Antonio. Her family had little money and lived in a succession of rented homes. Some were better than others, depending on the size of Frank's tips. The constant changes forced Yolanda to attend three different primary schools. Perhaps this is why ever since she was a little girl, her best friends have always been her brothers and sisters.

Yolanda was never very popular in high school, although she did have a boyfriend whom she dated for nearly three years. She passed her exams with good scores and was always dedicated and determined to do well. From 1979 on, when she graduated from McCollom High School, she dedicated most of her time to her college studies. In addition, she was soon faced with a major responsibility—she assumed much of the care of her brother's three children, who had been placed in his custody by the court. Despite this hardship, her nephews and little niece, who was also her goddaughter, adored her and she worshiped them.

In order to pay her way through school and help her parents financially, Yolanda worked for a time as a nurse's aide at a San Antonio hospital. She eventually received her degree in nursing in 1990, graduating with honors from the University of Texas Health Science Center in San Antonio. But it had taken her ten years to complete her undergraduate studies: Trying to work, study and raise three children was no easy task. She was the only one among her brothers and sisters to obtain a college education. This is why her diploma and her awards decorate the walls of the entrance to her parents' house. Her achievements are sources of pride for the entire family.

Once she obtained her degree, Yolanda held a series of jobs, working from sunup to sundown. At Saint Luke's Hospital, former co-workers remember her fondly as listening to her headset radio and humming along to the music as she went about her tasks. At one point she held two jobs at the same time. One was at a San Antonio hospice where she was in charge of taking care of patients with terminal cancer. The other one was at the San Antonio Chest Hospital where she covered the evening shift from 5 P.M. to 1 A.M., nursing patients with respiratory problems, tuberculosis and lung cancer.

A co-worker who shared duties with her in the emergency room would later point out Yolanda's dedication to her profession, adding that she never took her responsibilities lightly. As a nurse, she had earned the appreciation and respect of her co-workers. Perhaps that is why they collected money to buy her the clothes that she wore in court during her trial. By that time, Yolanda had lost so much weight that nothing she owned fit her.

Yolanda rarely dated, and when she did, it was neither serious nor lasting. Dedicated to her family and her work as a nurse, she became a solitary soul with a few close friends. However, there was something else that would soon fill her life and allow her to live out a fantasy.

In the middle of 1991, Yolanda saw Selena in concert for the first time. Yolanda was not a fan of Tejano music—she preferred country—until her niece invited her to the concert in San Antonio. She was quite moved. "When I saw her she lit up the stage," she told me later, her eyes shining as though she were seeing Selena at that very moment.

Yolanda Saldívar, it seems, had found something to be happy about. Like the truest of fans, she lost herself in her admiration for the talented and glamorous artist. Perhaps she was tired of focusing on her own mundane existence, the long period of hard work and study, the responsibilities of family. Now she had something new in her life, someone who, perhaps, she wanted to imitate in some way. Many believe that Yolanda lived vicariously through her idol and friend, Selena. In any event, that concert was a turning point in Yolanda's life—and those few hours would prove to be fateful ones for Selena as well.

Selena's performance had left such a powerful impression that after the show Yolanda looked eagerly for a concession stand where she could buy a souvenir to remind her of the singer. To her surprise there was not one single article for sale promoting the singer. And so the idea of a fan club was born.

According to Yolanda, she phoned Abraham Quintanilla only three times—not fifteen, as he maintained—and on the third try Selena's father agreed to a meeting. In any event, it is certain that they finally met to discuss the idea at the Club Reflex in San Antonio. Yolanda explained her intentions to Abraham; he seemed to approve and they reached an agreement. Suzette Quintanilla would be the contact person between Yolanda and the family, which is why Yolanda would not meet Selena in person until December 1991, six months after the club had been founded.

Organizing the club was a relatively simple task. In little more than three years, eight thousand people would join. In exchange for a twenty-two-dollar fee, members would receive one-of-a-kind products promoting Selena. Proceeds from the club would be donated to charity, and Selena's name would be associated with worthy organizations and causes.

Though she now held the fan club job, Yolanda kept working as a nurse, helping out her parents and living in the family's modest home forty-five minutes from San Antonio. The Saldívars have lived at that location since 1981, when Frank Saldívar invested his life savings to buy six acres of land for twenty thousand dollars. In 1992, their home caught fire and they lost everything, but the cruel blow did not lessen Frank's determination to provide for his family and continue to get ahead. Frank worked even harder at the restaurant while Juanita and her daughters made and sold floral decorations, from flower arrangements to funeral wreaths. Little by little, as they had done all their lives, they would buy secondhand furniture at the flea market. They themselves would repair the pieces, at the same time rebuilding their home room by room.

This tragedy did not affect Yolanda's relationship with Selena or with the Quintanillas. She could have asked them for help but she did not do so. Yolanda and her clan would forge ahead alone as always. Perhaps she thought it improper to ask for help from someone she barely knew, although the friendship between her and Selena was growing day by day.

There is no question that the admiration between Selena and Yolanda was mutual. According to several sources close to Selena, the increasingly successful singer had been feeling lonely for quite some time. Yolanda, another solitary soul but more mature than Selena, became her confidante and adviser. In addition to working on business matters, the two bonded through typical girl stuff, going to the mall, getting their nails done or simply chatting while they relaxed together.

Yolanda was proving to be the most efficient assistant that Selena could find. Whatever she wished for, no matter what it was, Yolanda would make it happen in some fashion. "If Selena would say, 'Jump!'" one source told me, "[Yolanda] would jump three times." Not surprisingly,

Yolanda eventually gave up her career in nursing to dedicate herself completely to the singer's enterprises, though initially she would earn less.

Selena's number one fan received tokens of affection from the singer, a kind gesture that she was not used to. Selena sent Yolanda cards expressing how much it meant to have her as a friend. When she found out that Yolanda had a collection of cow figurines, she gave her small presents with cow motifs.

Similarly, Selena had a passion for decorative eggs. Because she had been born on Easter Sunday, she'd collected Easter-related objects since she was a child. One thing missing from her collection was an egg-shaped ring. Perhaps that is why in December 1994, Yolanda presented Selena with a spectacular ring, valued at more than three thousand dollars. The bauble, designed exclusively for the singer, was topped with a Fabergé-like egg in white gold and surrounded with fifty-two tiny diamonds—almost two karats. The letter "S" had been worked in filigree on each side of the ring. Selena took such a liking to the piece that she had it altered to fit her index finger. That way whenever she would pick up the microphone to sing, everyone would be able to admire it.

There are receipts that prove Yolanda made the initial deposit on the ring using a credit card from the Selena Etc. boutiques. Fifteen days later she paid off the balance using another credit card from the business enterprise. Yolanda told the jeweler that the ring was a gift from the boutique's employees. This also was what Selena would say when asked about the jewelry. But Martín Gómez, the designer of

Selena's line of fashions, denied that money had ever been collected by the employees for that purpose.

So why did Selena refer to it as a gift from her employees if that was not the case? How could Selena accept such an expensive present without thanking those who worked for her? It is likely that the singer would have given her thanks in public for such a magnanimous gesture, in which case the charade would have been uncovered.

Later on when I interviewed Yolanda, she strongly hinted to me that the ring had not been a personal gift from the employees, nor was it a gift from Yolanda to Selena—she suggested it was part of a secret story. Yolanda does not deny that she paid for the ring, which was proven with sales receipts presented in court during her trial. However, she insinuated to me that it had not been she but a third party who had later taken care of paying off the credit card bill.

As you will see later, another key character in this complicated tale confirmed that Yolanda had been sent to buy the ring in order to throw people off the trail; this person also revealed to me the name of the supposed buyer. The ring acquired even greater significance when it fell from the singer's bloodied fist as she suffered in pain in the ambulance on the way to the hospital.

When I started my research for *Primer Impacto*'s trial coverage, I asked a detective friend to investigate Yolanda's past to see what he could find. His conclusions amazed many: Yolanda Saldívar was a model citizen, according to the investigator. The only offenses on record were fines for illegal parking.

When Yolanda's role is analyzed, the Quintanilla family offers different interpretations. Selena's siblings and her mother say that they never suspected a thing, nor did they notice anything odd about the fan club president's behavior. However, Abraham Quintanilla has presented versions that are contradictory. On a show broadcast by Univisión, he maintained that he had always mistrusted Yolanda. If that is the case, why did he consent to letting her create and run the fan club? Later, in comments made on Mexico's ECO network, Abraham said that when they were searching for someone to manage Selena's boutique it was he who recommended Yolanda for the position. How believable is it, then, that he would recommend someone he did not trust for such an important job?

It also does not seem certain that the Quintanillas did a background check on Yolanda. However, even if they had, they would not have learned the following: In the early 1980s, Yolanda was accused of having stolen $9,200 from the office of Dr. Faustino Gómez, where she worked. But the case was settled out of court, which explains why this episode never surfaced when my detective friend reviewed Yolanda's record. Whether they trusted her or not, what is certain is that the Quintanillas allowed Yolanda to get close to the family. I know there are home videos of the family in which Yolanda appears, sharing moments with them as though she were simply another member of the clan.

She was also one of the maids of honor at Suzette's wedding and is in the photos in the wedding album. When did the family's attitude start to change and why? Over the course of several months I was able to reconstruct the development of events that I believe unleashed the tragedy.

It all started in 1994 with the opening of the Selena Etc. boutiques—first in Corpus Christi, then several months later in San Antonio. As I mentioned earlier, it was Abraham Quintanilla who recommended that Yolanda be in charge of managing the stores' business affairs. But he could never have imagined what the repercussions of his decision would be.

Though Yolanda Saldívar appeared to be a competent administrator, some employees complained that she mistreated them and could be a difficult boss. I spoke with one former boutique employee who said that Yolanda was quite possessive in her relationship with Selena, constantly looking for ways to keep her away from the others. My source believes that Yolanda wanted to distance the singer from her employees to have more control over them and over Selena. But Yolanda argues that she merely wanted to be Selena's shield so that the singer would not have to worry about the petty issues that were part of running the business every day.

One of Selena's cousins who was also an employee of Selena Etc. recalls an incident during which she pointed out to Yolanda that certain receipts related to the sale of several items from the store were missing. Yolanda curtly responded, "That is none of your business." It could be that Yolanda had something to hide, but it is also likely that she found herself overwhelmed by administrative tasks for which she was not prepared and was hiding her inability by being authoritarian with others. Or perhaps she had everything under control and was fulfilling her role as manager, making the employees toe the line.

Another harsh critic of Yolanda's was Martín Gómez. He could not stand her and the feeling was mutual. The bad blood between them had been obvious for quite some time. Martín accused Yolanda of complicating the fashion work-shop's tasks by getting involved where she was not needed and of using Machiavellian tactics to get her way. According to him, Yolanda had established a reign of terror, even threatening the seamstresses with being fired if they did not side with her over him. Yolanda and Martín competed to endear themselves to Selena, each complaining to her about the other.

The hostility between them reached such an intensity that Yolanda began to tape Martín's conversations without his knowledge. She wanted to convince her boss that the designer was not looking out for the boutiques' best inter-ests. It is difficult to know if Yolanda wanted to get rid of Martín in order to protect her friend or if her goal was sim-ply a means to get him out of her way because she disliked him. In any event, Yolanda's behavior was questionable. Making tape recordings of him without his consent was playing dirty.

Yolanda wound up winning. Selena decided that she herself would start creating her own designs, which eventu-ally would put Martín in a supporting role. And little by lit-tle she would entrust her friend with more responsibilities. Yolanda had the key to her house, used several company credit cards, signed company checks, ran the fan club and often accompanied the singer on her trips. As Yolanda later told me, Selena assured her once, "When we triumph in Mexico, the success will be ours together."

Monterrey is the industrial capital of Mexico and is relatively close to Corpus Christi, about three hours by car.
Though on opposite sides of the border, the two cities share
a cultural wavelength and Selena was a popular celebrity in
both locales. Her desire to start a business in Monterrey was
not seen as out of the ordinary. Her dream was to mass market her fashion line, and a production facility in Mexico was
the first step in bringing her designs to life. She needed
someone who could devote time to developing her pet project, someone who was completely trustworthy and who
would support her unconditionally. Yolanda was more than
ready to play this role.

But in September 1994, something happened that
would completely change the relationship between Yolanda
and Selena. The singer met Dr. Ricardo Martínez.

Selena's concert in Monterrey had caused quite a sensa-
tion. That evening at a party to celebrate her success, her
uncle Isaac introduced her to the well-known plastic surgeon
who had recently operated on him. Dr. Martínez, married
and in his fifties, had his children with him. Selena exuded
her usual warmth, giving them her autograph and hitting it
off with Martínez from the very beginning. She loved the way
he spoke Spanish so well—exactly the way she wished she
could speak it. His elegance, his sophistication and, interest-
ingly, the stylish pony tail he wore caught her attention. It
was just the way her husband Chris wore his hair.

According to several people close to the singer and the
physician, a special relationship between Ricardo and
Selena started to grow from that moment on. She began to
entrust him with her most intimate thoughts. She even told

him that her marriage was not going well since she felt that her husband did not support her in her goal of launching her clothing business. Ricardo filled that void. He had contacts in Mexico to help her get the factory going and to avoid the bureaucratic processes typical of that country. He became her financial adviser.

He also became her doctor. When Selena decided to have a contraceptive implant removed from her arm, she called on Ricardo. On another occasion, he performed liposuction on the singer. Yolanda had to settle with tending to her friend and taking care of her after the operation, giving her massages to prevent air bubbles from forming under her skin. Yolanda was not at all happy that her friend was coming to depend more on Martínez and less on her. She was quite perceptive and immediately knew that she was losing control of the situation.

Selena started to travel to Monterrey more frequently, sometimes wearing a disguise. Sebastian D'Silva, who was then Dr. Martínez's assistant, picked up Selena several times at the airport. He says that at times she would wear a wig so that people would not know who she was, even using Pérez as her last name as an added measure of anonymity. On one of those first visits to Monterrey, Selena found her hotel room filled with flowers, a welcome present from Ricardo. This gesture did not sit well with Yolanda, who had accompanied Selena on the trip. She warned the singer to be careful because she believed the doctor had other, less professional intentions.

It was widely known that Abraham Quintanilla was totally opposed to the idea of Selena carrying out her plans to manufacture clothes in Mexico. He did not want her musical career to be relegated to second place since it was the family's principal source of income. Besides, he thought it risky for his daughter to launch more business enterprises than she already had, especially when one took into consideration the fact that the boutiques were not doing well.

Selena had been forced to reduce the number of employees of Selena Etc. from thirty-eight to fourteen due to a lack of profits. Checks were being returned unpaid by the bank because the boutiques' account lacked sufficient funds. And as Dr. Martínez explained when he spoke with *Primer Impacto* months after her death during an exclusive interview, at one point he had to lend several thousand dollars to Selena because she was short of cash. In the long run, Quintanilla wanted to protect his daughter. But the singer, just like her father, was hard-headed and determined to make her dream come true. Selena had decided to find her own way, even if she defied her father in the process.

Perhaps in his heart and soul Abraham believed that his daughter did not wish to behave so rebelliously, that *someone* was a bad influence. For him that someone seemed to be Yolanda. The instinctive reaction of almost any parent faced with a situation like this is a desire to blame others for their children's behavior and to protect them from that negative force. Maybe that is why Abraham began taking a closer look at Yolanda and then attacking her mercilessly.

Although the boutiques' business was declining, Selena's musical career was thriving. The last time I saw Selena was February 6, 1995, less than two months before her death. Miami's Calle Ocho Carnaval put its best foot forward to welcome her. And spectacularly. Though she was not yet as well known in Florida as she was in Texas and elsewhere, she instantly won new fans in Miami with her appealing stage presence and music. I remember her as very charming with a beautiful, sensual smile. This tremendously talented woman (who was only the warm-up act that day) would shatter numerous album sales records in a matter of months—for Selena's music would prove to be more popular after her death.

The real draw that day was a woman considered to be the number one entertainer in the Latin world—Thalia, star of the hit Spanish-language soap opera *Marimar*. When she sang that day at the Calle Ocho Carnaval she captured everyone's attention. Selena, although an important presence, was not the main attraction. However, this did not concern the queen of Tejano. What worried her was something else entirely: Selena was concerned about her rival, not as an artist but as a competitor in the fashion industry. Thalia was also in the process of launching a line of clothing. Selena wanted to be number one in that world, which is why she rushed the preparations to begin production at the facilities in Mexico. Months later in an ironic twist of fate, Thalia would host a Univisión special on Selena, an emotional posthumous homage.

During late 1994 and early 1995, Yolanda frequently traveled to Monterrey, presumably to expedite the factory project. The plans were coming together despite Yolanda's claims: Suspicious vehicles were following her on her trips, the air had been let out of her car's tires and Abraham Quintanilla had started to threaten her.

The black clouds of trouble were casting their shadow and the storm that would destroy the lives of the two women was taking shape. Abraham increasingly pressured his daughter to distance herself from Yolanda, even going so far as to tell Selena that her friend was a lesbian. It was during that period that Armando Saldívar had a falling out with his sister Yolanda for reasons he did not wish to make public.

In an exclusive interview with *Primer Impacto* months after Selena's death, Armando said he felt guilty for something terrible he had done as a result of his argument with his sister. Blind with anger he supposedly made up a story that Yolanda was stealing funds from the fan club and told none other than Martín Gómez. Delighted to have more ammunition to battle the woman he hated so much, the designer wasted no time in telling one of Selena's uncles, who, in turn, told his brother, Abraham Quintanilla. Armando Saldívar told *Primer Impacto* that he felt tormented with regret. His words sounded sincere, but his reasoning did not seem logical. The Saldívars were a very close family. No matter how angry he might have been with his sister, it does not make sense that Armando would have taken his revenge in such a damaging manner.

In any case, this piece of gossip was the straw that broke the camel's back for Abraham. He apparently had noted certain irregularities in the administration of the fan club and claimed that some fans were writing him letters complaining that they had sent checks for twenty-two dollars in return for promotional materials about Selena that they had never received. This would have been Yolanda's direct responsibility. Now, armed with the information he had gotten through Martín Gómez, Abraham had the perfect excuse to confront Yolanda.

On March 9,1995, he called Yolanda to a meeting at which Suzette and Selena were also present. This event signaled the beginning of the end. Selena's father cornered Yolanda, demanding that she explain the matter of the fan club finances and why the club members were not getting their gift packs. According to Abraham, Yolanda dismissed the complainers as fans who were trying to get something for free, but this explanation did not convince him. After listening to her he threatened to land her in jail for being a thief. The following day, Yolanda, for unknown reasons, showed up at Abraham's offices at Q Productions and the singer's father ordered her to leave the building. By this time, Selena was deeply troubled by the conflict that had erupted between two people so near and dear to her. Her father, with his charges against Yolanda, had successfully planted some seeds of doubt. Yet Selena knew for a fact that her best friend and right hand was continuing to work hard on the Monterrey project. How could Yolanda be betraying her? She seemed to be giving her all to get the factory up and running.

On March 13, Yolanda sought the advice of a lawyer and together they composed a letter addressed to Selena in which Yolanda tendered her resignation as an employee of Selena Etc. The letter made it clear that her decision was due to the harassment she was suffering daily at the hands of the Quintanilla family; she also asked for payment of any salary and expenses due to her.

Was the letter a ruse? Perhaps Yolanda wanted to manipulate the singer, knowing that Selena had mixed feelings and thinking that after her resignation, her friend would turn against her own father for meddling in her affairs. Then she would ask Yolanda to continue working for her. Or perhaps Yolanda was sick and tired of her efforts not being appreciated and of Abraham's threatening her and really did want out of the situation. Whatever her motivation, what is certain is that her letter of resignation was found in the purse that Selena left behind at the Days Inn on the day of her death.

On March 13, the same day that the resignation was drafted, Yolanda bought a .38 caliber revolver. Yolanda would later say that she bought the gun because for quite some time she had been receiving death threats from Abraham. (Eventually, she would give three different reasons for purchasing the gun, including this one.) What is truly odd is that a few days later she returned the weapon, claiming that her father had given her another one. Then on March 26, Yolanda returned to the same store to repurchase the revolver.

If we accept as valid that her fear was caused by the threats, then why the indecision in the purchase of the gun? Does her attitude express doubts about how useful having a gun would be? Or does it symbolize changes of heart in those who threatened and protected her? According to Yolanda, the hesitation was due to Selena's begging her to get rid of the weapon and to the supposed promise to protect her from her father. After Selena made her request and her promise, Yolanda would return the gun.

We do know for a fact that that particular .38 was the weapon used to kill Selena and that the person who fired it was Yolanda Saldívar. The revolver cost $232 dollars. The bullet that snuffed out the star's life was barely worth 25 cents. The police never found the bullet.

According to Yolanda, during the weeks prior to March 31, Selena would hide her in one hotel or another to prevent Abraham from finding out that they continued to be friends and were still working together on the Monterrey project. When these allegations came out during the trial, I called the hotels Yolanda had named and found that she had indeed stayed in them on the dates mentioned and had been seen occasionally in the singer's company. But it seems that Selena reached a point when she could no longer put up with her father's pressures. Yolanda herself admits that her friend later requested that the two of them remain apart for a while to allow Abraham to calm down.

It was shortly after this period that Yolanda told Selena she had been raped during her trip to Monterrey. Could it be true? Or was it another one of Yolanda's schemes, like the ones Martín Gómez had referred to, to make her friend feel pity for her and not abandon her?

By now, Yolanda was no doubt disturbed at the turn of events in her life. On one hand, there were the ongoing battles with Abraham; on the other, she felt cast aside by her friend since, despite her warnings, Selena maintained her involvement with Dr. Martínez and was determined to get the clothing factory in Mexico up and running—with or without Yolanda—and start a new phase in her life. In fact, three people close to the singer told me the same story separately: Selena wanted to divorce Chris and had made this clear to her husband and that she wished to move to Monterrey.

The singer had already visited a house that she would rent in the Colonia del Valle neighborhood of that city at 113 Rio Guadalquivir Street. It was two stories tall and contained three bedrooms. Leticia Sinta, the sales coordinator for the real estate company Century 21, told *El Norte,* a Monterrey newspaper, that the initial contact for the rental had been Yolanda and that the queen of Tejano herself was about to close the deal. "All this took place in February of 1995 and we were ready to finish up with the last details, to the point where all we had to do was sign a few papers," confirmed the sales agent.

But Selena would never get to live there. The clouds were about to burst and the violent storm was on the verge of engulfing her completely.

5

The Corpus Christi Hearings

AUGUST 1995

Two months before Yolanda's trial, I flew to Corpus Christi for the preliminary hearings. I arrived three days before the first hearing because I had landed two exclusive interviews: one with Dr. Vicente Juan, the doctor who supposedly had attended to Selena as she lay dying; the other one with the Saldívar family. I kept my trip as secret as possible to prevent other members of the media from finding out and trying to scoop me on the interviews.

But who could have predicted it? I had just set my bags down in the hotel room when I learned that both interviews had been canceled. Dr. Juan was accessible and willing to speak, but the public relations spokeswoman at the hospital advised him that he should seek permission from the victim's family before speaking to the media. Abraham's response was firm: No way, out of the question, he said. I called Abraham myself to speak with him about his position, but he yelled at me: "You, the press, will always do anything to get a bigger audience." I was livid, but I stood my ground. "First of all, don't generalize," I began. We spoke for an hour and he finally calmed down, but he refused to give his consent for my interview with the doctor.

The Saldívar interview had also been canceled. Arnold García, one of the members of the defense team, called, somewhat embarrassed, to tell me that all had been brought to a halt. It seems Yolanda had not been able to sleep the night before for fear that her family would say something that would enrage Abraham and cause him to threaten them, too. Yolanda had given her consent for me to meet with her family and we had made our arrangements a week earlier through Garcia. I had rearranged my schedule to arrive early, and now I was facing three wasted days in Corpus. Over time I would discover that Yolanda would tend to change her mind at the last minute.

Arnold invited me to dinner so we could talk about "important things." I was not sure what he was referring to, but curious, I agreed to meet him at a restaurant near the bay. He easily recognized me because he had seen me on TV. I would never have recognized him because he was wearing a pair of shorts. He assured me that Corpus Christi lawyers tend to dress more casually than those in Miami.

Over a drawn-out dinner and countless cigarettes, I did what I could to get information out of him. He, however, was looking out for his client. He seemed to want to cooperate with me, but he would only offer anecdotes and facts with a spin that favored his cause. At the end of the meal, when he realized how frustrated I was due to the canceled interview, he invoked an old Spanish saying. There is no direct translation, but roughly it's the equivalent of "You have to open a lot of oysters before you find a pearl." I realized then that I had to be patient. From the start, Arnold and I would get along well; he knew what I wanted and I understood what he was trying to do.

In Corpus, the key to our coverage was to keep one principle in mind: respect. Respect for the public, who we were obligated to inform to the best of our abilities; respect for the victim's family—humble and hardworking people who were living through their darkest hour; and respect for Yolanda Saldívar, who had yet to be proven guilty. I made a commitment to honor this principle through my reporting, steering clear of coming out for or against a particular verdict.

I put the canceled interviews behind me and turned my attention to the events about to unfold in Corpus Christi. We carefully studied the meaning of the preliminary hearings so that we could explain their significance to our viewers: Preliminary hearings take place in court prior to jury selection. During this phase the judge rules on motions presented by lawyers on both sides; the objective is to handle various requests in advance so that the trial is not delayed, including deciding what evidence will be allowed into the court and which witnesses will be called. Preliminary hearings define the parameters of a case and clarify the charges. At *Primer Impacto,* we decided to broadcast our coverage of the hearings live from outside Nueces County courthouse building.

On the first day of the hearings there was another trial of sorts—a trial by fire for the Saldívar family. When Yolanda's family reached the courthouse, they huddled into a tight group with their arms around each other as though trying to protect themselves. And for good reason. My colleagues from other media organizations literally had them up against the wall, aiming their cameras and microphones at them like a firing squad pointing their weapons at its victims.

I watched everything from a distance. Although I had several cameras available, I decided not to add my microphone to the barrage. Not only was it unnecessary at that moment, but the entire scene seemed cruel and grotesque to me. Yes, I understood these camerapeople and reporters were simply doing their job, as I have done on numerous occasions, but in this instance it was overkill. The Saldívars were visibly uncomfortable with the attention and totally vulnerable. Their only help came from Jamie, a friend of Yolanda's, who ruined all the camera takes by holding a paper fan in front of the family members' faces. Except for "the witch with the fan," as the press christened her from that moment, the Saldívars were alone without any support and were being needlessly pressured and scrutinized.

I'm sure the family was waiting for me to join in the attack, but I did what they least expected that morning. I smiled at them but kept my distance, trying to let them know that my attitude was clearly different from that of my colleagues. They saw me and responded, nodding their heads in approval. In fact, Jamie herself, who turned out to be a very nice person, would open up to me later on. That first day, like everyone else, she was tense.

In any case, there was very little the Saldívar family could say publicly. Yolanda's lawyers had instructed them to restrict their comments to a written statement, which had been drafted so they would not say anything that would jeopardize Yolanda's case. The statement asked the press to refrain from asking the family any questions because the Saldívars wanted Yolanda to get a fair trial.

In the following days I noticed an obvious change in the family's attitude. The Saldívars started to greet me with a wave of the hand. I would respond, but took great pains not to get closer to them in any way. I did not want them to feel pressured by me. Then one morning as I left the ladies' room I bumped into María Elida, Yolanda's older sister, and their mother, Juanita Saldívar. While María Elida thanked me for my respectful attitude, Juanita blessed me and thanked me for having conducted my coverage in a balanced fashion. Then María Elida revealed something that shocked me: "Yolanda asked me about you," she said with a mischievous smile. Evidently I was winning the family's trust.

Later that same day, something unexpected happened in the courtroom. All the seats were occupied, including those that were assigned to the press. As I walked to my seat in the first row, I realized it was already occupied—by Abraham Quintanilla! The seats assigned to the two families were occupied primarily by the Saldívars. Since Selena's father refused to sit near the family of the accused, he took the only empty seat in the press section, which happened to be mine. When I reached my place I politely asked him for my seat. He yielded it gracefully. During this embarrassing scenario, he asked a security guard in a whisper where he could sit down. But his greatest fear had become a reality. The officer pointed to the row assigned to the victim's family, right in front of the Saldívar family. That's when I heard something that I'm sure no one else heard. Selena's father hissed, "I'm not sitting with those people!" And for lack of other options, he was forced to leave the room.

The Saldívars were seated far enough away so that they were not able to hear what had been said. They only managed to watch the mini drama and how it appeared that Abraham had been forced to leave because of me. I believe they might have interpreted the event to mean that I was on their side. But in truth, I had no other motive than to do my job well from the best seat in the courthouse, which by chance was mine.

That afternoon was full of surprise encounters. In addition to my close brushes with the Saldívar family and Abraham, I ran into Douglas Tinker in a courthouse hallway. It was a brief and polite meeting. Perhaps he did not remember, or did not want to remember, that a few days earlier he had hung up on me after our tense phone conversation. There were two things about him that caught my attention. One was his sheer physical presence; the other was the dandruff the size of snowflakes sprinkled over his shoulders.

Back in the courtroom, we listened as the preliminary hearings unfolded in Judge Mike Westergren's courtroom. Since the prosecution insisted that Yolanda had killed

Selena after being confronted with theft, the first step the defense took was to attempt to discredit that particular motive. But to do so they would need the fan club's financial records. They made a motion requesting these documents. Tinker presented as his witness the young woman who had replaced Yolanda as fan club president. In her testimony, Irene Herrera verified that she had given five books containing the club's accounting information to Abraham Quintanilla. Westergren ordered Abraham's lawyers to make all these documents available.

Tinker also requested that all financial records of Q Productions be made available as well as all the personal tax forms he had filed with the Internal Revenue Service. Abraham's lawyers responded by requesting that this motion be denied. Indignant, Selena's father told the press that his lawyers' request did not mean he had anything to hide. Tinker, he said, was simply trying to derail the hearings and was sidestepping the real objective: to try Yolanda Saldívar for the murder of his daughter.

Ultimately, the court decided that Abraham's personal financial records were not relevant to the case. But it seemed that the defense was using the shotgun approach to see what they could catch. Perhaps that is why they made a motion requesting Selena's criminal record, if there was one. Of course they came up empty-handed. The request I found most interesting was Tinker's motion asking for the medical records detailing Selena's liposuction operation in Monterrey. I saw it as a legal maneuver by Yolanda's lawyers to be able to call on Dr. Martínez to testify. But they were wasting their time. When Martínez gave his deposition voluntarily by phone from Monterrey, he did not say anything of consequence. And his deposition was never used during the trial. The doctor's more controversial comments would come months later.

As the hearings wore on, everyone expected that Tinker would claim his client had suffered from temporary insanity and had committed the crime after losing control. But the attorney did something quite different and stunned all of us in the courtroom. He promised to show that what happened on March 31 had been a regrettable accident. The courtroom was in shock—no one had even contemplated the possibility that Yolanda might be innocent. Tinker went on to reveal, for the first time, his client's version of events: Yolanda supposedly had tried to commit suicide after arguing with Selena in room 158. The singer then opened the door to go get help. Holding the gun in her hand, Yolanda gestured for Selena to close the door. It was at that moment, according to the defense, that the gun went off by accident. Silence filled the courtroom.

I was not entirely surpised by Tinker's move. A few days earlier during my dinner with García, he sketched out some general points of their courtroom strategy without violating his lawyer/client confidentiality, and I suspected they might try to use an accident defense. García knew that many members of the press were prejudiced against Yolanda from the start, a frustrating position for him to be in since the media would influence public opinion of his client, and I believe he was trying to find allies for his cause. He was convinced that his client was innocent and wanted to convince me as well.

At one point, *Primer Impacto* also figured in the hearings. The court requested access to the April 4 video that we had aired of Rosario Garza, the maid at the Days Inn who was said to be an eyewitness to the crime and who claimed to have heard two shots and to have witnessed Yolanda gunning down Selena in the motel hallway. The defense wanted to convince the judge that the young woman's comments on our show had prejudiced the potential members of the jury against their client, making it impossible to conduct a fair trial. Tinker also requested all records of any psychiatric treatment Garza might have had, trying to prove that perhaps she was not emotionally stable enough to testify. Garza was subpoenaed to appear at the hearings but she would never be called to testify. She appeared to be quite nervous. When I spoke to her outside the courtroom, I asked her if she still stood by everything she'd told us in her interview. She did, but this time she provided a detail that was truly incredible: "I saw the bullet enter [Selena's] back and come out the front. I saw it as though it was in slow motion."

For me she lost all credibility at that point. Maybe Superman can see a moving bullet, but Rosario Garza could not. Besides, thanks to my contacts at the police department, I knew the ballistic report concluded that Yolanda's weapon had been fired only once, not twice as Rosario had maintained. Blood had been found in the motel room, not the hallway. Selena had been shot once, in room 158. Either Rosario was lying or she thought that she'd witnessed something that she couldn't possibly have seen.

Even the head of my department, Alina Falcón, had her moment in the courtroom. She was representing

Univisión along with the corporation's lawyers, petitioning the judge to allow the use of cameras in the courtroom. This way the trial would be transmitted live to our audience. Cameras in the courtroom would have given the viewer the opportunity to observe the judicial system at work, including learning how a verdict would be reached, no matter what it might be. Unfortunately, the judge was firmly opposed to the idea. I'm sure he had nightmares that his courtroom would become a circus like the O. J. Simpson trial, which had just ended.

Tinker's next step was to try to throw out the confession that his client had signed in her own handwriting on the night of her arrest. This piece of paper was truly a deadly weapon in the hands of the prosecutor, because in it Yolanda confessed that she had committed the crime and never mentioned the word "accident." To support his cause, Tinker called Detective Paul Rivera to testify. It was Rivera who along with another officer had obtained the confession from the accused after a long interrogation.

Rivera has worked with the Corpus Christi Police Department since 1978 and has a solid reputation. As soon as he sat down on the witness stand, Tinker began his attack. He got him to admit that Rivera's brother was an old army acquaintance of Abraham Quintanilla's, and that, hanging in his own office, was a poster of Selena, a gift from the Quintanilla family. Tinker was trying to prove that the detective had a conflict of interest.

The defense maintained that the confession had been obtained illegally because legal counsel had not been present, despite the fact that Yolanda had requested it. Tinker also added that his client had been pressured unnecessarily since she had not been allowed to eat, have a drink of water, go to the bathroom or see her family until she signed the confession. Under these circumstances she could not make decisions clearly. According to Tinker, Yolanda insisted that her statement include the word "accident"—something the officer chose to ignore—and she finally agreed to sign the document without the key word because she was exhausted from the standoff in the parking lot.

The defense also managed to get Rivera to admit that after obtaining Saldívar's confession, he destroyed every single note he had taken during her interrogation. He said it was his habit to do so.

In her confession Yolanda explains how Selena's business had been going downhill and how they had had to drastically lay people off in the previous months. She mentions that Abraham accused her of being a lesbian and a thief. Then she reveals that during her recent business trip to Monterrey, she had spoken with Selena by phone and that the singer had asked her to bring her certain bank statements and financial documents in her possession. When Yolanda returned to Corpus Christi on March 30, Selena made a brief stop at the Days Inn to pick up the requested documents, and Yolanda seized the moment to tell her friend that a man had tried to rape her in Monterrey and showed her the bruises from the supposed attack.

The following day, March 31, Yolanda says Selena took her to the hospital for a medical examination. When they returned to the motel, Selena told Yolanda she had given the financial documents to her father, and he claimed that the papers were "wrong." Yolanda became upset and told Selena she did not wish to work for her any longer. They argued. Yolanda describes what happened then: "I took the gun from my purse and Selena started walking toward the door … I pulled the hammer back and I shot at her as she was walking toward the door, which was open."

It did become clear in court that after signing the statement, Yolanda was allowed to see her father for a few minutes. Then she was put into a jail cell.

When the prosecution questioned Rivera, the officer denied having committed any irregularities. Valdez, the prosecutor, backed up this testimony by presenting another document signed by Yolanda, in which she admits that the officer informed her of her legal rights before her interrogation. Yolanda's signature is barely legible. The handwriting is shaky—possibly indicating that she was close to her breaking point.

The prosecutor continued to defend Rivera's reputation by pointing out the changes Yolanda had made to the confession in her own handwriting before signing it. None of the changes made by the accused includes the word "accident." If the events that really took place were different, why did Yolanda agree to sign a declaration full of lies that clearly implicated her? Or was she in fact pressured into signing?

Tinker, who is sometimes called the poker player due to his risk-taking but often effective courtroom strategies, certainly lived up to his nickname when he played another unexpected, high-stakes card: calling Robert Garza, a Texas Ranger, to the witness stand. The Texas Rangers have a reputation for being truthful and steadfast supporters of law and order, though a generation earlier they were feared and hated by many Mexican Americans throughout the state for their bullying tactics. But those days are over and now, ironically, a Texas Ranger of Mexican descent would be taking the stand to defend a Hispanic woman, Yolanda Saldívar.

When he walked into the courtroom, Garza commanded everyone's attention. The handsome Garza stood over six feet tall and wore an impeccably tailored western-style jacket. His impressive bearing left many of the women in the audience breathless. His voice echoed against the walls and sounded convincing.

Garza had witnessed part of Detective Rivera's questioning of Yolanda. Although he was not with them in the room where the interrogation took place, he could see everything that was taking place from an adjacent room equipped with a one-way mirror. The purpose of such a room is to allow investigators to study the behavior of the suspect. On the opposite side of the glass from Garza, Yolanda and Rivera could only see their reflections in a mirror.

Although the interrogation room is supposed to be soundproof, the Texas Ranger claims to have heard snatches of the conversation in which Yolanda assured Rivera that the whole thing had been an accident, and watched as she told her version using dramatic gestures to describe how the gun had gone off.

Eventually, Garza asked Rivera why he had not included the accident version in Yolanda's confession. Rivera responded by reminding Garza that murderers tend to create excuses so that they do not have to accept any blame for their actions. From the beginning, it was obvious that Garza was uncomfortable testifying against a colleague—an officer with whom he had investigated a number of cases. After hearing the words of the Texas Ranger, the defense successfully left the impression that Detective Rivera had acted as prosecutor and judge toward Yolanda.

As soon as Garza finished speaking, I set my mind on getting Officer Rivera's reaction for my afternoon show. Apparently fate was on my side, because I had just left the courtroom when I found Rivera by himself, waiting for the elevator. I quickly approached him to ask for an exclusive interview. He seemed very doubtful and asked me if I worked for any of the local stations. By his tone I immediately realized that the last thing he wanted was to see himself later that day on a Corpus Christi newscast. After all, he had not had a good day in his hometown. But I was determined to land the interview to make the coverage complete, so I answered without lying and without going into great detail. "No, I'm a journalist from Miami."

As soon as he heard that, he was no longer reluctant to speak to me. The truth is that my show is broadcast by the network from Miami and is seen not only in Corpus Christi but all over the state of Texas, from coast to coast in the United States and in a dozen countries in Latin America. No, I didn't feel guilty because I had omitted these details. If I didn't grab him, surely some other journalist would have.

As soon as he agreed to the interview, I went into "stealth mode." When we went down together in the elevator, I was more than certain that my competitors waiting around the courthouse door would see me leave the building with someone, and suspect that I had landed a prize interview. It would be impossible to prevent them from tagging along and it would cost me an exclusive interview. I asked Rivera to walk a few steps behind me to the parking lot as though he did not know me. In this manner, walking through the gauntlet of journalists and equipment with my brightest smile on my face, I was able to tell María López in a whisper, "Go get a cameraman and follow me discreetly." My producer, who was used to turning on a dime, was able to get Ivan, a cherished colleague who was both quick and efficient, to set up his equipment.

We were ready in an instant, and I wasted no time in beginning the interview.

"What's your opinion of the declarations of the Texas Ranger's statements?" I began.

"The Texas Ranger is wrong," he answered, now nervous, as he got ready to get into his car.

"Are you sure?" I asked him, afraid he would get away.

"I'm certain."

"Did you change Yolanda Saldívar's confession?" I asked, hoping to halt his departure.

"No."

"But the Texas Ranger claims to have heard Yolanda say that everything was an accident," I reminded him as he visibly became even more nervous.

"That's not possible," he answered. "He was outside the room and he couldn't hear anything. It's impossible to hear anything through that mirror."

I knew I only had a few seconds left, so I decided to be quick and straightforward with my questions. He was the same way with his answers.

"Yolanda Saldívar never told you that it was an accident?"

"No."

"Yolanda Saldívar never told you that she wanted to commit suicide?"

"No."

"Yolanda Saldívar never told you that she fired the gun without meaning to as she motioned to Selena to close the door?"

"No."

Paul Rivera rarely looked me in the eye, and he gave the impression that he was uncomfortable with all these questions. This would be the only time that he spoke to the press during the hearings. (What's rather curious is that instead of hating me, he apparently took a liking to me. Months later, when he found out that I had gotten married, he told a mutual acquaintance that he was heartbroken.")

The hearings moved along. Tinker was determined to get the judge to change the trial venue, arguing that it was unlikely his client would get an impartial jury in Selena's hometown. Selena's death had become international news and nowhere did she have more friends and fans than in Corpus. It was the only topic of conversation. To bolster their position, the defense presented a former Nueces County judge as a witness. She was clear and firm in her support for a change of venue, claiming that the chances of "little green men coming down from Mars" were greater than the chances of Yolanda's getting a fair trial in that city.

Sure enough, on the day these arguments were being heard, a radio show in Corpus Christi conducted a survey and the results were two to one, with the majority of the public agreeing that there would not be a fair trial if it were held in Corpus Christi. Fifty-two percent of the inhabitants of Corpus Christi are Hispanic and that community was convinced that Yolanda was a cold-blooded killer. Finding twelve impartial jurors would have been difficult in any part of the state, but in Corpus it would have been impossible.

On the last day of the hearings, the judge announced his decision on the two most important motions. Tinker managed to get the trial moved to Houston where the percentage of Hispanics is 28 percent. When Westergren announced the change of venue, he did it in a low voice, in an almost indifferent manner. Many people asked each other if they had heard correctly. We would soon discover it was the judge's habit to announce key decisions as though he were talking about the weather.

But though Tinker had won on that score, Carlos Valdez achieved his own victory. The judge rejected the defense's request and allowed Yolanda's confession to stand as evidence. With this document in hand, it wouldn't matter whether the trial was in Houston or on another planet inhabited by the little green men. A written, signed confession would make it very difficult for any jury to exonerate Yolanda.

With these decisions, the stage was set for one of the most important trials in the history of the Hispanic community.

6

Waiting

Yolanda Saldívar awaited her trial in anguish, rarely touching food. During the six months she spent in jail in Corpus, she hardly ate. Her weight plummeted from 156 to 105 pounds and her dress size went from 16 to 8. Every day she would lose a few pounds. A few days before her trial began in Houston, her former hospital co-workers from San Antonio gave her some dresses to wear, but even the smallest ones hung loosely on her frame. She used a decorative pin to gather the extra fabric in an attempt to make the dresses fit better.

I learned this from Yolanda's sister, María Elida, during one of our long phone conversations. Shortly after the hearings in Corpus Christi, she began to open up to me. One day, she called to give me the family's new phone number. They had to change it after the hearings—the press was driving them crazy. They did not wish to be interviewed and reporters were calling them night and day, making her parents quite nervous. She gave me the new number after getting permission from Yolanda, whom they consulted on everything. I realized I had won their trust, and I was deeply grateful for this gesture. I never gave the number out, even after the trial was over.

On another occasion, María Elida called me—upset because Yolanda had been found to have breast cancer. I was surprised and asked her several questions about the news, but all her answers were evasive and abstract. I never mentioned it on my show out of respect and consideration for the family. Later, I asked María Elida once again about her sister's state of health. I wanted to know how it had all turned out. She answered me rather indifferently, "I don't know; it looks like nothing's wrong." Now I feel free to write about it because I don't believe the diagnosis was ever real. I think Yolanda invented it so I would pity her and that she used her sister as a tool to get the message to me. The incident tells me a lot about Yolanda's need to control and makes it easy for me to believe that she used the same tactics to manipulate Selena.

In the weeks before the trial, which was scheduled to start in October, Yolanda's lawyers were preparing for battle. A new member was added to the team—Fred Hagans, a high-profile personal injury expert who would be handling his first criminal case. He was so enthusiastic that he brought not only his professional expertise but also his money to the preparation of the defense. The case was generating huge amounts of publicity and surely the investment would be worth every penny. Tinker's team staged a mock trial using a jury chosen by an expert. The rehearsal cost Hagans approximately twenty thousand dollars.

They arranged to rent a courtroom equipped with video cameras to record the proceedings. Tinker presented his arguments and theories to the jurors. When the verdict came in, one third voted to acquit Yolanda. But much to his surprise, the rest accepted the confession she signed in front of Paul Rivera as valid.

We tried to map out our strategy as well. First of all, it was imperative that we have on-air legal analysts who would be able to help us interpret and report upon every aspect of the trial. *Primer Impacto's* producers were able to hire two Texas legal experts who would make events as clear as possible for those of us not familiar with the law and its intricacies. I was lucky that my colleagues were able to find Jorge Rangel, a former judge, and José Castillo, a well-known Houston defense attorney. Throughout the long weeks they described what steps were being taken in court, offered their opinions and explanations and went so far as to debate between themselves the pros and cons of each legal maneuver. Their analysis and broad range of comments seasoned our coverage like salt and pepper.

On the air, I constantly referred to them as "the former judge from Texas" and "the prominent defense lawyer," so they would be easily distinguishable to our viewers. At critical moments, they actually wound up reporting for us, dra-

matically relaying testimony from the courtroom like veteran journalists. They were naturals, and by the time the
trial ended, Rangel and Castillo found themselves giving
autographs. We spent many hours arguing, hypothesizing
and discussing different theories, becoming close friends in
the process.

Rangel and Castillo deserve the acclaim they received
not only for their technical proficiency, but also for their
unflagging professionalism. I found out from a reliable
source that a legal analyst hired by a competitive network
had been instructed to slant his commentaries in favor of
Selena. Not only did I find this unethical; it was also
shoddy news production. In a sense, we *all* favored Selena,
for she'd been the victim of the ultimate crime. But we
were covering a trial. If for any reason Yolanda were to be
found innocent, the public deserved unbiased coverage
that would explain precisely how that particular verdict
had been reached.

The night before the trial was to begin, we went all the
way. We managed to produce a live special out of the
Houston courtroom where the jury selection would take
place in a matter of hours. Thanks to some negotiations on
the part of our executive producer, we were the only members of the press allowed access to this facility. We even used
a special crane to raise and lower a camera, obtaining a
bird's-eye view of the entire courtroom. My cohost on the
show, Myrka Dellanos-Loynaz, was broadcasting her por-
tion of the show from the Days Inn in Corpus Christi.
Without her providing this angle, it would have been
impossible to have provided such complete coverage.

I opened the broadcast with an important revelation. Since I had good contacts with the prosecution team, I found out that Carlos Valdez was not going to present Rosario Garza as a witness due to the number of contradictions in her testimony. I placed my hand on the witness stand for added drama as I announced the exclusive news: "*Primer Impacto* sources confirm that Rosario Garza, supposedly the only eyewitness to the crime, will not be called by the prosecution to testify, since her version would have contradicted the other witnesses at the motel as well as the police reports." Indeed, later we would find out that she never set foot in the Houston courtroom.

In the broadcast, I was also able to show the seating arrangement for the 182 seats available. There were 76 for the press, 8 for the courtroom artists, a section for the victim's family and the family of the accused, and the remaining spaces—anywhere from 35 slots on up, depending on how many family members showed up—were for the public, assigned through a lottery each morning.

Our cameras were able to show how the mood in the city was becoming ever more tense on the eve of the trial. Three gangs—one in Houston, one in Miami and one in Los Angeles—made a bet to see which one of them would be the first to kill Yolanda if she were to be found innocent. People on the street demanded that she be declared guilty and be given the maximum penalty.

Our live edition proved to be quite popular with viewers, but none of us were prepared for the impact the broadcast would have. As part of the show, we had prepared an elaborate dramatization of the crime. It was almost like a brief movie, depicting all the events—every known version of them—leading up to that moment on March 31 at the Days Inn. The preproduction took on the quality of a Hollywood feature, complete with a casting call, where we chose actors who most resembled the players in this drama—Yolanda, Selena and Abraham. And we found locations similar to the original ones. We were very careful, though, because dramatizations or reenactments can certainly distort reality. So we were as faithful to the evidence as we could be. There were no inventions or exaggerations. Everything was based on court documents.

At one moment, our filming almost came to a halt because "Yolanda" broke her arm on the set. Many of us were hard at work in the newsroom when we heard, "Yolanda is in the hospital." There were those who thought that she had gotten beaten up in jail, or that something worse had happened, until someone confirmed that it was Yolanda, the actress. She continued playing her role with her arm in a cast, and the final takes had to be done by carefully placing the camera in order to avoid showing her arm. We finished editing the piece in the nick of time, right before we went on the air. The effects were so realistic that one of the cameramen told me, "It's incredible. It looks like a movie. I feel like I was there and that I witnessed what happened." That night, when the one-hour special was over and hours before the beginning of the trial, our viewers knew that *Primer Impacto*'s coverage would be unequaled.

When the show ended, the controversy began. It must have been very hard on Selena's family to witness a dramatization of her shooting—and it must not have helped that the scene was so faithfully re-created. Abraham Quintanilla criticized our dramatization and unfairly questioned the veracity of the events we had presented, but he was not content to leave it at that. He called a press conference at the offices of KQQK, a Houston radio station, to condemn the Hispanic media in general, alleging that their coverage distorted events. When he realized that someone from a competing network was present, he became quite angry and refused to continue until she left the room. When he was told that a *Primer Impacto* cameraman was present, he demanded that he be kicked out.

The English-language press was anxious for the press conference to begin, but they did not support Quintanilla in his censorship of the Hispanic journalists. They sensed that in the future they might be the ones to be picked on if they said something that did not please him. The incidents were caught on camera and aired that night on many local newscasts throughout the state of Texas and elsewhere.

The controversies did not end there. During our special, we strongly promoted a Selena-themed program that Cristina Saralegui, the undisputed queen of Hispanic talk shows, would be presenting following our broadcast. She had asked me to be on the show, along with our two legal experts, to speak about the case against Yolanda. Abraham had also been invited but, due to his outrage at our special edition, he threatened to cancel *Cristina.*

Cristina wanted him as a guest because his presence guaranteed high ratings. Every time Selena's family had made an appearance on her previous shows, this had been the case. She managed to calm him down and he agreed to go on. I had no idea of how the show was going to be conducted. Shortly before it began, I called Cristina on the phone to reassure myself that there was not going to be a confrontation on the show. I also wanted to ensure that in case Abraham was to make accusations against us, that it be explained to him, with all due respect, that what we had done on *Primer Impacto* was based on information obtained from court documents. In other words, I gave my colleague all the ammunition she needed in order to defend us, if that were to be necessary.

Rangel and Castillo, who would also be on camera with me on *Cristina*, showed up in front of the Houston courthouse. The show is taped at Cristina's studio in Miami and we would be on air live through a satellite feed, able to hear the show's transmission through the IFB. When we were ready for the show to begin, we heard the tail end of a conversation in which Cristina said to Abraham, "Thanks for your trust, Abe." Rangel and Castillo, who were by my side, also heard her comment. The three of us looked at each other and we crossed our fingers, hoping that everything would turn out all right.

The show began and I did a recap of the legal proceedings up to that point, telling a few stories about our coverage. I finished up and the show continued from Miami. Then Abraham, who was also doing the show from Houston via satellite, had his opportunity. He complained about what he had seen on our show, and Cristina let him talk for a reasonable amount of time so he could vent his feelings. Then in a very professional manner, she changed the topic. Shortly after that point, she had her own confrontation with Abraham; in the middle of the show, he found out that the author of an unauthorized biography of Selena was also on the program, and he blew up. During the commercials, he abruptly got up from his chair because he did not want to be on the same show with the writer. Once again, Cristina soothed him and managed to hold him back for a few minutes so he could at least say good-bye to the viewers, who were told that he had to leave due to prior commitments.

Quintanilla's outbursts with the media repeated over and over. My friend John Quiñones, correspondent for ABC's *Primetime Live,* told me that "interviewing him was a real headache." Abraham drove the producers crazy with his requests and conditions. His behavior extended to print media as well. When a *Newsweek* photographer went to photograph him for an article, Quintanilla tried to persuade him to sign a release so that all rights to the photo after its initial publication would belong to Abraham. *Newsweek* refused. The press would also be annoyed by his demand that all questions be submitted to him in writing prior to the interviews.

Despite all this, we at *Primer Impacto* never held a grudge against Abraham. On the contrary, from the beginning we wanted to sit down at the table with him and discuss his concerns about our dramatization. We even offered him an interview in which he could air his complaints.

He agreed to speak on our show only if he was allowed to choose the interviewer. He requested Mauricio Zeilic, who at that time was host of a segment on my show. Surely, he must have thought, since Zeilic was the entertainment reporter, he wouldn't be quite as inquisitive as an investigative journalist might be (such as I would have been). Or perhaps he had fond recollections of how kind Mauricio had been when he had interviewed Quintanilla shortly after Selena's death. Whatever his thoughts, we considered his demands a bold attempt to manipulate us. My boss, Alina, remained steadfast on this matter and I respect her for that. Finally, Abraham Quintanilla canceled the interview.

With time, his behavior changed. It is only fair to say that he was extremely open and kind when I finally interviewed him on December 1, 1995, after the trial was over. Of course, by then he had reason to believe in my integrity. During that interview, he answered all my questions and was not closed to any topic.

After his numerous run-ins with the media, many networks chose to present coverage of Abraham's arrogant treatment of their journalists. I was approached by reporters in search of controversial comments, but they wouldn't get any from me. Univisión executives made their policy totally clear: "We're not going to argue with a father who is mourning the death of his daughter, no matter what he might say." I was proud to work for a company that knew how to handle such a delicate situation with so much class.

Just before the beginning of the trial, our energies were also focused on trying to get an exclusive interview with Dr. Martínez. When we at last contacted his office in Monterrey, we were referred to his lawyer. When we contacted his legal adviser, he said, "My client's time is very valuable and he needs to be compensated in some fashion." He never mentioned a sum, but it was obvious that he wanted money.

This really annoyed me. We do not pay for interviews on my show. It is a matter of principle. People who charge for interviews have been known to exaggerate, embellish or even make up stories so that interviewers feel satisfied that they have gotten their money's worth.

Weeks later, Martínez would change his mind and talk to us without compensation. Perhaps his lawyer was testing the waters when he spoke to my producer and hinted that his client should be paid in order to agree to an interview. But by not setting any conditions, Martínez's testimony had much more credibility. He said many interesting things in his interview—which you will read about shortly—but I will tell you now that he is certain that he was the last person to have spoken to Selena, minutes before she went to meet Yolanda on that fateful morning at the Days Inn.

The Trial

OCTOBER 1995

On the first day, I sensed that there was something amiss in the courtroom, but I could not put my finger on what was wrong. After glancing at the crowded group of spectators several times, I realized that a man seated in the center row—one reserved for the public—was creating some kind of a disturbance.

He was poorly dressed and unshaven, with a crazed look about him. Although there were enough seats in the courtroom, several people chose to stand in small groups rather than sit next to him. "It's because he stinks," I was told by a colleague, once word had reached all the way to the press section. I turned around again and saw him lost in his own world. I realized he was a homeless man. Who could have imagined? The trial of the decade in Texas, the judicial event most closely followed by Hispanics in the United States, was about to begin and inside the courtroom, where no cameras were allowed, the people's main concern was the personal hygiene of a luckless homeless man.

"He's not as unlucky as you might think," I was reassured by a female spectator wearing pink satin pants. "They caught him trying to sell his entry pass, but the guards made him stay." I soon found out what had happened. The homeless man had slept on the street and had happened to awaken on the very corner where the public was required to wait each morning for the lottery-awarded seat assignments. The officer in charge thought the man was an obsessed Selena fan who had camped out on the corner, determined not to miss the first day of the trial. He happened to be the first one chosen, and when he saw the other selected people cheer as though they had hit the jackpot, he thought that they were giving away breakfast inside the courtroom. And so, at this moment, there were people outside fighting to get in, and here was a man who wanted to leave because he discovered that the courtroom was not a cafeteria.

The morning of October 11, 1995, was the first time that the public and the media were allowed in the courtroom. But in reality, the trial had begun two days earlier with the selection of the jury, which took place behind closed doors. My colleagues and I were able to follow events of the jury selection because the judge allowed for a court reporter to give a briefing after each session.

I held in my hands the mile-long questionnaire that had to be answered in writing by those called upon by the county. Among many questions, they were asked if they were members of Selena's fan club, if they had attended her funeral and if they were capable of granting a verdict in favor of the accused even though it might not be popular to do so in the community.

In order to pick jury members that would potentially favor their cause, the defense was counseled by Robert Gordon, a jury specialist who had been a consultant in another much-publicized case, the trial of William Kennedy Smith. Smith, nephew of Senator Edward Kennedy, was found innocent of the charge of raping a woman at the Kennedy's Palm Beach, Florida, compound. Douglas Tinker and his team were looking for people who did not have blind faith in the police and who were open to the possibility that an officer might lie, even under oath. They also wanted people who believed that a weapon could go off accidentally.

The prosecution, on the other hand, searched for a more conservative panel made up of people who knew how to handle weapons and were convinced that they could not go off accidentally. They also wanted people who had their own businesses and, at some point, had had to lay off employees.

Tinker was quite agile in disarming potential jurors. With seemingly trivial questions, jokes and anecdotes, he was able to lower their defenses and managed to have them reveal their true feelings about the accused. At that time, when the collective hate toward Yolanda was palpable, the defense surprised the jury candidates by asking each one to stand up, look the accused in the eye and tell her to her face that they considered her innocent until there was proof to the contrary. Most of them could not do it. It was an efficient way to get rid of the "undesirables" since those who had any doubt at all were removed immediately.

The law is quite clear: A person is innocent until proven guilty. Several prospective jurors said they had already formed an opinion about Yolanda, which automatically disqualified them. A large percentage said they were opposed to the law that allows for a conditional probation for someone convicted of murder if they had no previous criminal record—which would be the case for Yolanda. This also eliminated them from the panel.

Eventually, the twelve jurors chosen included seven Anglos, four Hispanics and one African American. At *Primer Impacto,* we asked Chris Ben, a jury specialist who had been involved with jury selection for the O. J. Simpson trial, for his assessment. After a thorough analysis of the jury profile, Ben concluded that the majority of the jurors were somewhat or very conservative, which would benefit the prosecution.

In front of the TV cameras, both sides stated that they were satisfied with the choices, but I knew the truth to be different. The defense would have preferred more African Americans and fewer Hispanics, for obvious reasons.

Judge Westergren gave instructions to the jury, ordering them not to discuss the case amongst themselves, not to watch TV, read newspapers or listen to the radio. It was a tall order, but standard in every jury case and an obvious necessity. The trial was the main topic of conversation seemingly everywhere, and Westergren did not want to resort to having the jury sequestered.

On the day that jury selection was over, there was a surprise. Ricardo Vela, our star reporter and my good friend, came looking for me, breathless after a long run. María Elida, Yolanda's older sister, had just run into him on a street corner near the courthouse and had asked him to find me right then and there so she could be interviewed. Finally a family member was going to break the silence!

I was in front of my computer in the Univisión trailer, wolfing down a sandwich, and dropped everything and ran. María Elida had agreed to speak with us as she sat inside her car, but she was afraid of death threats that her family was receiving and requested that we cover her face on-screen. So we did. And that finally earned me her trust, because it convinced her that I kept my promises. Later on she let Yolanda know this. That afternoon she talked to us as she cried, and her words were deeply touching.

She was worried about her sister. "She's weak and sad," she said. "She cries a lot. Whatever evil was done here was done by Abraham Quintanilla. My sister is not a monster. We're humans, we're Catholics. I know the Virgin is going to help us. It's not true that she's a lesbian. Just because she never got married does not mean she's a lesbian. I'm not married. I'm forty-five years old, and I'm not a lesbian. What happened is that she dedicated body and soul to her work. The relationship between my sister and Selena was that of two good friends. She was like our little sister."

Later she sent a message to the person she felt was to blame for all this: "Mr. Quintanilla, I hope you feel shame and regret for the pain you have caused so many people." Off camera, María Elida told me that during the days prior to the trial, her family, scared, "had been hiding in a secret place in Houston so that no one could find them." I felt very sorry for them. The night before the trial was to begin, María Elida still spoke affectionately about Chris, Selena's widower. She had not realized that the relationship between them could never be the same—Chris was going to testify against her sister. I had the feeling that for the Saldívars, the clock had stopped in a happier time, and they were not aware of the magnitude of all that was happening.

At the end of the interview, drying her tears, María Elida told me that a TV network had offered her four thousand dollars for an exclusive interview, which she had refused. Indignant, she told me her reasons for her decision. "What do they think … that my family's dignity has a price? Not for a million dollars would I speak with someone who would later turn things around and endanger my sister's case."

Back in court Wednesday morning, I forgot about the unfortunate homeless man and watched as Westergren entered his courtroom, solemn with its cedar woodwork and the imposing Texas flag draped above the judge's bench. There was no question that the decor had been thought out to reinforce the strong presence of justice.

I saw the prosecution team arrive early, carrying boxes and boxes full of documents. There were so many cartons that they had to use a small cart to transport them, though despite the amount of materials, the lawyers and their assistants appeared to be very organized. Carlos Valdez wore a small lapel pin, a little silver angel, for good luck. It was a gift from his wife since it so happened that the trial had begun on his forty-first birthday. He wore the pin every single day of the trial.

I had been one of the first journalists to arrive, because I wanted a seat that allowed me to clearly see everything that was happening. Outside, the security measures were almost extreme: There were dozens of policemen with police dogs to sniff out explosives. Before being allowed to enter the building, each person was required to go through several X-ray machines to detect any concealed weapons. And all credentials allowing access to the trial were carefully examined by the officers.

In addition to dealing with the people entering the courthouse, the police also kept an eye on the huge crowds that were beginning to gather outside. Though only a handful of spectators were allowed into the courtroom, mobs of people waited patiently outside each day of the trial, making clear their feelings about Selena and the woman accused of murdering her. They held up posters and photos of their idol and handmade signs, some quite elaborate. There were also hundreds of specially created Selena T-shirts and hats. Most people supported the prosecution and were determined to express their opinion of Yolanda; all were loyal fans of Selena.

When I went up to the fifth floor and entered the judicial chambers, I discovered that the accused was already seated in her place, dressed in a red jacket and a gray vest and speaking with Arnold García. After a while, Yolanda whispered something into his ear, and then he pointed at me. She turned, looked at me and each one of us made a slight gesture of recognition. It was the first time we had seen each other face-to-face. Later I found out that she had asked Arnold if I was present in the courtroom. I'm sure she was curious to find out who the reporter that she had seen on television was and who had written her more than twenty letters during the last few months. She must have been intrigued by that insistent person who would not accept no from her lawyers, nor her silence.

Gradually, the other players in this tragedy made their entrance. Perhaps I never noticed so clearly the differences between one family and the other. Every member of the Quintanilla family was there. They even hired a spokesperson to handle the press. The Quintanillas were a well-dressed and sophisticated-looking clan. The Saldívars were represented by María Elida and her mother, Juanita, who was holding on to her daughter's arm. Both were dressed in humble clothes and they looked fearful, as if beaten down by life and by having to bear the unbearable. But the two families had one thing in common: the sad, pained expressions they wore on their faces.

When Abraham Quintanilla entered and sat down, the tension in the courtroom was palpable. Yolanda turned to one side to look at the jury, as if to avoid any exchange between them. At first, Abraham did not pay any attention to the accused, but when the charge of murder in the first degree was read aloud by the court, he gave her a fearful, fiery look that seemed difficult to ignore. Yolanda then entered a plea of not guilty.

The opening arguments got under way immediately. Valdez recounted the prosecution's version of the events in a simple way, getting right to his point, but he did so in a monotonous tone of voice without dramatic pause or emphasis. The jury appeared to become bored, with one of the twelve actually nodding off. The prosecutor described Selena's death "as a simple case of murder" in which the accused, with one gunshot, had severed one of the victim's main arteries in two, causing her to bleed to death. He wrapped up his opening argument by stating that the court and jury were about to embark on a "journey in search of justice." As he spoke, Juanita Saldívar prayed in a low voice.

Then Tinker began his presentation and woke everyone up. His narrative and emphasis of particular words were like those of a professional storyteller describing the plot of a mystery movie. According to him, the film's lead was Abraham Quintanilla. Describing him as a controlling and dominating father, ambitious for power and money, he denounced Abraham for having pulled Selena out of school to make her sing in bars and nightclubs for the sole purpose of making money. He emphasized that Quintanilla's control was so great that he made his family live in a sort of compound, the better to watch them. (Chris and Selena lived next door to her parents, and the families' houses were surrounded by a fence.) He painted the family environment as stifling and Selena as someone who was fighting to become independent. Tinker maintained that the singer wished to make a break from her father's control and open her own businesses. For that she had counted on the help of Yolanda Saldívar, who in turn had received death threats from Abraham for that very reason.

I looked toward the bench where the Quintanillas were seated while the defense attorney continued with his grave accusations. And there was Abraham, visibly uncomfortable, subtly shaking his head and occasionally looking up at the ceiling as if he couldn't believe his ears. He was burning up inside.

The defense repeated what they had stated during the hearings in Corpus Christi: What happened at the Days Inn had been a tragic accident.

According to Tinker, Yolanda ran after her friend to help her after the gun went off. That's why she got into her truck—to search the motel's surroundings. When the lawyer finished, A.B. looked indignant, shaking one foot from side to side as though he had a pebble in his shoe that irritated him.

It was time for the prosecution's first witness, and they would begin with Abraham Quintanilla.

Wearing his ever-present dark sunglasses and emanating an innate strength, he walked toward the stand. Raising his right hand high, he swore to tell the truth. The courtroom was perfectly quiet as Valdez, in a soft, almost fatherly tone, began to interrogate him. Quintanilla's serious demeanor fell apart when the prosecutor showed him a picture of his daughter and asked him to identify her. From that moment on, Quintanilla's voice kept breaking and we all felt the heartrending pain of a father who'd lost his child. He became so nervous that he could not remember important dates, such as when Selena and Chris's wedding had taken place.

Then the prosecutor asked a series of questions that appeared to be totally unrelated to the case and that amazed everyone.

"Did you have sexual relations with the accused?" asked Valdez, receiving a firm no from Quintanilla.

"Did you rape the accused?" he continued.

"Of course not!"

No one understood the reason for this line of questioning, but it would become clear days later.

Finally the prosecutor touched upon the alleged theft of funds from the fan club. With total conviction, Quintanilla insisted that Yolanda Saldívar was a thief. Valdez asked his witness to identify the person he was accusing if she were in the room. Firmly and with almost uncontainable fury, Abraham pointed his index finger at Yolanda. At that moment she rose from her seat slowly, without taking her eyes off Quintanilla. It was a defiant gesture. She wanted everyone to see that she no longer feared Quintanilla and that she had nothing to be ashamed of.

Tinker began his cross-examination and asked Abraham why he had not provided the fan club's financial records since he was accusing Yolanda of misusing the funds. Abraham, tense and defensive, interrupted Tinker several times, raising his voice. This was one of the few times that Westergren had to call for order.

Chris Pérez was the next witness. He looked tired, with bags under his eyes. He said that he, as well as his wife, had not trusted Yolanda for a long time before the crime. I looked at María Elida and saw her blinking rapidly, as people tend to do when they can't believe what they're seeing with their own eyes. For her, at that moment, Chris came tumbling down from his pedestal.

Kyle Voss and Mike McDonald, two employees of A Place to Shoot in San Antonio, testified next. They worked in the gun shop and shooting range where Yolanda had bought the revolver. Each described how when Yolanda went to the store for the first time, she told them that she was a nurse and needed a firearm to protect herself against a patient's relative who was threatening her. That day she left a deposit and returned two days later to pay off the balance and pick up the .38 caliber weapon. They instructed their unusual customer in how to fire the gun since she clearly did not know how to use it. Two days later, Yolanda went back to the store to return the weapon, because supposedly her father had given her another one. To their surprise, Saldívar returned eleven days later to repurchase the gun. It was March 26—only five days before the tragedy at the Days Inn.

During the cross-examination, the defense got Mike McDonald to admit that when someone cocks back the hammer on a .38 caliber revolver—as Yolanda had done when she intended to commit suicide inside room 158—the gun can go off with just a touch. In fact, McDonald said that it takes less pressure to fire a weapon in "single action mode," when the gun is cocked and the hammer is ready for firing, than it does to turn off a light switch.

For eight straight years, Selena Quintanilla Pérez dominated the Tejano Music Awards, becoming the queen of Tejano music. [ALEXANDER FRANCO/MANNY HERNANDEZ]

These six photos from a short video sequence taken at a Selena Etc. boutique opening just a few months before the murder show just how close Selena and Yolanda had become. Though only twelve seconds long, the video shows Selena confiding in or perhaps sharing a secret with Yolanda, whose expression goes from concerned to amused. [COURTESY KORO CHANNEL 28, CORPUS CHRISTI, TEXAS]

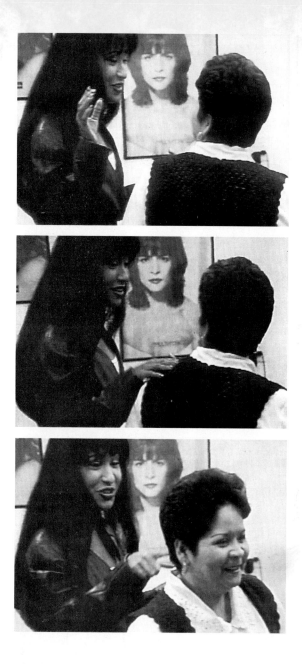

*D*r. Ricardo Martínez, the enigmatic Monterrey plastic surgeon who would come to play a large part in Selena's life. He is allegedly the last person Selena called before departing for her fateful meeting with Yolanda.

$\mathcal{Y}$olanda Saldívar at the helm of one of the Selena Etc. boutiques several months before the murder. [COURTESY KORO CHANNEL 28, CORPUS CHRISTI, TEXAS]

$\mathcal{T}$he mysterious ring that fell from Selena's hand as she was being rushed to the hospital. According to Yolanda, the ring is a part of the "secret."

[COURTESY KORO CHANNEL 28, CORPUS CHRISTI, TEXAS]

[NORMA JEAN SIERRA]

[NORMA JEAN SIERRA]

*D*uring the trial of Yolanda Saldívar, the courthouse was surrounded by angry fans demanding justice and by more sorrowful ones, like the three mourners in the center photo who each carried a white rose, Selena's favorite flower. Some, like the woman pictured on the next page, called for 100 YEARS FOR YOLANDA; others sang her songs, cried out for justice or simply called for Selena.

[NORMA JEAN SIERRA]

$\mathcal{T}$he day after: Disbelieving fans gathered at the Selena Etc. boutiques to share their grief and erect impromptu shrines to the memory of their fallen idol. Similar shrines were erected at Selena's home in Corpus Christi, at the cemetery and in front of the Days Inn motel room where she was shot.

*T*he attorneys for the prosecution: Carlos Valdez, right, and Mark Skurka prepare for a press conference. Valdez, who grew up in the same Corpus Christi neighborhood as Selena, is wearing his silver angel lapel pin. His wife gave it to him for good luck and he wore it every day of the trial without fail. [NORMA JEAN SIERRA]

*D*ouglas Tinker, the famous criminal lawyer who headed the defense team, and Arnold García, to his left, another of Saldívar's attorneys. [NORMA JEAN SIERRA]

*D*efense attorney Fred Hagans, a high-powered Houston lawyer who joined the defense team.
[MARIA CELESTE ARRARAS]

$\mathcal{T}$he author with Univisión's legal analysts: Jorge Rangel, a former Texas judge (center), and the prestigious defense attorney José Castillo (right). The photo was taken in the alleyway studio of *Primer Impacto* minutes before the start of a broadcast. [MARIA CELESTE ARRARAS]

$\mathcal{A}$ typically chaotic scene outside the Univisión trailer at the courthouse. In the distance one can see the alleyway studio covered by a white canvas. This section was closed to the public during the trial and always full of journalists and police. It was also used for the press conferences given by the prosecution and defense. [MARIA CELESTE ARRARAS]

$\mathcal{M}$aría Celeste during her exclusive interview with Yolanda Saldívar in which Yolanda revealed Selena's secret. The two are looking at a letter that, according to Yolanda, she received from a psychic with a message regarding Selena. [MARIA CELESTE ARRARAS]

$\mathcal{F}$rank Saldívar, Yolanda's father, who is very active in his church community. He is shown here at the courthouse with Father Richard McCarthy from San Antonio. He accompanied the Saldívars to Houston as a gesture of support. [NORMA JEAN SIERRA]

$\mathcal{T}$he author interviewing Selena's father, Abraham Quintanilla. It was during this interview that Quintanilla showed the author documents that suggested Yolanda had been embezzling money from the Selena Etc. boutiques. [MARIA CELESTE ARRARAS]

$\mathcal{A}$lmost a year after the murder, Abraham Quintanilla, wearing his ubiquitous dark sunglasses, poses for a publicity photo during the casting call for the movie of his daughter's life. The young girl in the foreground was hoping to portray Selena as a child. [MANNY HERNANDEZ]

$\mathcal{I}$n what must have been an eerie moment, Selena's mother, Marcella Quintanilla, greets one of the more believable look-alikes. [MANNY HERNANDEZ]

Selena, radiating the beauty and poise that made her one of a kind. [MANNY HERNANDEZ/ALEXANDER FRANCO]

Selena's husband and bandmate, Chris Pérez, at right, at Univisión's 1996 Premios Lo Nuestro, the Latin world's equivalent of the Grammy Awards. He is seated with Selena's brother, A.B., the man who composed the songs that his sister brought to life. [MARIA CELESTE ARRARAS]

Selena onstage.

(MANNY HERNANDE)

A shot of Selena taken outside the Univisión offices in Miami before an interview with *Primer Impacto*. Apparently, Selena liked this photo so much that she had it enlarged and displayed prominently in her home. [EMERITO PUJOL]

That afternoon at the end of the session, Tinker publicly promised that Selena's name would not be dragged through the mud in his arguments. It was a respectful move, but more than that, an intelligent one. The fervor of those who remembered Selena was so strong that at this point she was worshipped almost as though she were a saint. To have said anything against her reputation would have been suicidal.

Thursday, the next day, was a tough one for the defense. The witnesses were the employees of the Days Inn, the nurses who attended Yolanda after the alleged rape in Monterrey and some of the employees of Selena's boutiques. The most moving moment came when the motel janitor, Trinidad Espinoza, claimed to have seen Selena run out of the room with Yolanda chasing after her, pointing the gun at her back. Using a diagram of the motel's layout displayed in the courtroom, Espinoza pointed out the path that Yolanda allegedly took while chasing the victim. He described how Yolanda suddenly came to a halt, lowered her pistol and, displaying no emotion, returned to her room.

These words left the jury hypnotized and chilled the rest of the courtroom, but no one had the same reaction that Selena's mother did. Marcella Quintanilla could not take it. Almost fainting, she had to leave the courtroom. Shortly after, she was hospitalized with chest and arm pains due to a sudden rise in her blood pressure.

Norma Marie Martínez, a cleaning woman at the motel, came after the janitor. She described the same scene as Espinoza, but she added something unexpected: that as Yolanda followed her victim, she was yelling "Bitch!" at

Selena. This whole new dimension—that something was said during those final, terrible moments—made the scene even more dramatic.

Curiously, Norma Marie's version was different from the one she had presented months earlier in front of our cameras at *Primer Impacto*. At that time, she maintained that as Yolanda chased Selena, Selena was screaming for help. But she said nothing about the cussword. She also had not reported this to the police in the beginning.

The prosecution tried to explain this discrepancy as best they could. According to Valdez, the witness omitted the word in her original version simply because she was embarrassed. She was ashamed of saying it in front of the police and even more embarrassed to say it on TV.

Be that as it may, at that moment her claim was too important for Tinker to ignore. He asked the cleaning woman to point out the exact place where she was standing when everything had happened. When she did so using the diagram, the lawyer easily made it seem doubtful that she could have heard the word, since she was standing at a considerable distance from the vicinity of room 158. (Later Tinker would bring out another witness who also refuted Norma Marie's version.)

The parade of witnesses for the prosecution continued that afternoon. The employees of Selena Etc. maintained that their boss had been questioning Yolanda because the financial picture was looking so grim. Celia Solís, a manicurist at one of the boutiques, said that on the afternoon before her death, Selena said she planned to fire Yolanda as soon as she got back certain financial documents from her.

The nurse who had seen Yolanda early on the morning of March 31 and hours before the tragedy had occurred also testified. Patricia Biggs said that she was not able to determine if the patient had been assaulted sexually because she had not performed a vaginal examination. The alleged assault had taken place outside of Corpus Christi, not only in another city but in another country, and Yolanda was a resident of San Antonio. If Yolanda wanted to file a complaint, she had to do it in San Antonio or in Mexico.

Biggs explained that during the visit to the hospital, Yolanda said she had bled only a little and that Selena appeared to be upset with Yolanda because earlier her friend had told her privately that she was bleeding copiously. It seemed to the medical staff that Yolanda was lying to Selena about her condition.

In his cross-examination, Tinker asked the nurse to describe the patient's mood in the hospital. Biggs pointed out that Yolanda barely spoke and kept her head lowered, looking down at the floor as if she were depressed.

"Aren't these symptoms of depression consistent with those of a victim of sexual assault?" Tinker asked. The nurse agreed, and the defense scored a point as they attempted to prove that Yolanda had, in fact, been assaulted.

Karla Anthony, another nurse, testified that Yolanda was curled up in a fetal position. She added that Yolanda had red welts on her neck and arms, although in her opinion they did not resemble bruises received from a baseball bat, which was what Yolanda said had been used to assault her.

The prosecution brought out the clothes that had been torn during Yolanda's alleged rape. The moment she saw these, Juanita Saldívar seemed to age on the spot. The poor woman, clearly shaken, had to leave the courtroom.

But the prosecutor remained unmoved and proceeded to demonstrate how, in his opinion, the tears in the pants and shirt did not seem consistent with an assault. Instead, it seemed that they had been shredded purposely with a pair of scissors. The prosecution was obviously trying to prove that Yolanda had not only lied about the rape, but had also planned everything to make it seem real.

In the recaps that were aired that afternoon, we all agreed that the day's testimony had been lethal for the defense. But none was as deadly as that of Trinidad Espinoza, who, with his clear details of the chase, had moved the jury. But aside from his testimony, his simple and humble manners, as well as his honest appearance, seemed to give him a lot of credibility. He had nothing to win or lose by presenting his version of the events.

There's no question that the following day, Friday the thirteenth, would also be unlucky for the defense. The reception desk employees at the Days Inn testified, painting a pathetic portrait of what were probably the last few moments of the singer's life. Rosalinda Gonzalez, the assistant manager, told the jury how "Selena entered the reception area bleeding, clutching her chest. When we asked her who had shot her, she said 'the girl in room 158.'" Ruben De León, marketing director for the motel, described a similar scene. "Selena said, 'Yolanda, Yolanda Saldívar shot me. The one in room 158.'" The receptionist, Shawna Vela, said that she had heard the same thing as the other witnesses, but added that shortly before Selena collapsed, she heard her scream, "Lock the door!" Shawna says she asked the singer "Why?" and Selena responded with "Lock the door! She'll shoot me again." These were key words, because the victim, before her death, told us that someone was trying to kill her with "intention"—and intention must be proven in order to convict someone of murder in the first degree. Shawna's testimony left us frozen in our seats, especially when she said, "I saw so much blood I felt nauseous. Selena fell to the floor. I called 911."

However, there's a fly in the ointment. Shawna Vela said that she had called 911. But on the recording, you can clearly hear the noise she made as she hurriedly looked through the motel records to find out who was staying in room 158. Why would she look for the identity of the occupant if she and the others present had supposedly heard Selena name the alleged assassin? Was she lying?

The prosecution tried to explain these inconsistencies using common sense. "Sometimes four people in the same room see or hear the same thing, but in different ways," said Mark Skurka, who was conducting portions of the interrogation for the prosecution.

Someone who saw something entirely different was Sandra Avalos, a former motel maid who testified that she had seen Yolanda chase after Selena. But unfortunately for the prosecution, the woman she described to police did not resemble Saldívar. During cross-examination, the defense pointed out that according to Sandra, the woman chasing the singer was of medium height and had bleached-blond hair with dark roots that needed a touch-up. Yolanda has dark hair and is tiny, barely measuring four feet nine inches.

The day ended with the testimony of the paramedic who had come to Selena's aid at the Days Inn. Richard Fredrickson said, "I pulled off her clothing, looking for a wound, and I saw a hole in her chest." He explained that her veins were dry due to extensive blood loss. In the ambulance he was the first person to notice the presence of the mysterious ring that fell from the singer's hand: the Fabergé egg.

The first week of the trial reached its end. The prosecution undoubtedly had emerged as the star player, covering much ground on their journey in search of justice: The victim's father had cast doubt on Yolanda's honesty; the accounts of the Days' Inn employees suggested that a crime had been committed with intention, and in cold blood; and the paramedic's testimony, which included details of the victim's physical agony, added the final dramatic, if somewhat morbid, touch. The defense would have a long road ahead.

We were all exhausted. Our team was producing one or more news briefs every hour, two *Primer Impacto* shows a day (one for the East Coast and one for the West Coast) and a special coast-to-coast edition nightly. I had to divide my time between the courtroom events and the live broadcasts. There were not enough hours in the day. On Friday, I hopped on a quick flight to Miami to see my family. It was a mini marathon, but I was able to "unplug" somewhat. Home was an oasis for me, and I looked forward to returning to my husband, Manny, and Bella and Chula, my two dogs. Even so, the tension of all the coverage followed me back to Miami—with comic consequences.

In the midst of preparing my shows and the madness prior to my departure for the trial, I was having the outside of my house painted. Ordinarily, I would have picked the color and checked daily on the progress, avoiding the common error of choosing a paint shade that looks good on paper but not too convincing on the walls. I thought a light peach was the ideal color and Manny left the job in my hands to please me. In the merry-go-round of the days prior to the coverage, I could only see the "work" at night through my exhaustion. On my return from Houston I realized the magnitude of my error. My house was like a giant pumpkin, stem and all, because on top of everything the window frames and other details were painted green! The moral: Never paint your home while you're doing something else that's important.

Although I now needed sunglasses to look at my house, my home was the best therapy against stress. Working, actually living, under pressure for almost four weeks in a transmission trailer, trying to concentrate, surrounded by cables and computers, eating each meal quickly and sleeping three to four hours a day can drive anybody crazy. In order to deal with this makeshift lifestyle, the forty of us from Univisión sent to cover the events pinned photos of our loved ones on a large bulletin board. This huge collage of parents, fathers and mothers, children, husbands, wives, girlfriends, grandchildren, boyfriends and, in my case, dogs had almost become an altar. But it could never take the place of the warmth of the people (and pets) that we most loved.

When I returned to Texas, I spent a lot of time doing more than searching out information and preparing for the shows. A good part of my day was dedicated to reciprocating the kind gestures I received from the public. I took turns with my on-air colleague from Univisión, María Antonieta Collins, greeting our viewers who would gather together for the chance to meet us. Even so, that was not enough—we received all kinds of gifts, even the most incredible love poems. There were silly as well as profound questions about the trial, the show and our personal lives. And, of course, there would be the never-ending autographs. I signed Selena T-shirts and posters which, without a doubt, was quite an honor for me. People would offer me precious images of their idol to autograph, so I was touched to be asked to sign them. I also wrote my name on hats and baby clothes. I would say to parents, "I really don't want to ruin his pants," but they would insist. "But that's why we brought them, so that you would sign them and we could keep the memories." Incredible. I was quite moved.

At every opportunity, I would step out to greet our viewers, but I could not always make the time during the especially busy days. That is why some of them waited for hours until I left the courtroom or completed a broadcast. When I would go to put on my makeup and change my clothes in one of our trailers, they would follow me. They would peek through every single crack, and I would become paranoid, closing every curtain so they wouldn't catch me undressed or in the bathroom. I received some of their photographs later by mail, leaving me with fond memories of those days. But thank God none of them were X-rated!

I never felt worthy of so much attention. On the contrary, I felt that I owed something to these people. After so many years in television, I'm still surprised by the impact, the reach and the power of this medium. Nowadays, I spend most of my time inside the studio speaking to a camera, with the technical team at my side. It's still hard to believe that at that very same moment while I'm talking to a piece of equipment, there are millions of people looking at me. I speak to those on the other side of the lens as though I were speaking with my friends. And that's why when I see them on the street, the connection with viewers is so natural. I feel they know me and that I know them, and this was certainly the case in Houston.

The second week of the trial contained all the elements of a soap opera: accusations of rape, death threats, suicide attempts, surprise tactics and allegations of police conspiracies.

Monday started out like a bomb going off. As we listened to the tapes made during her negotiations with the police, we were transported to the pickup truck where Yolanda had held her siege. The vehicle had a cellular phone, so it had been possible to record the conversation.

When the tapes were played for the jury, the courtroom became perfectly silent while Yolanda's voice, with its almost unbearable tone of agony, filled the air: "I want to kill myself! I don't want to live anymore!" Eerily, her howls were also heard in the press trailers parked outside the courthouse, since they were equipped with a communications system that would allow them to hear the audio from the courtroom. It was hair-raising.

Officer Larry Young used a thousand and one strategies to keep Yolanda from carrying out her intention of killing herself. With a fatherly tone, he begged her to take the gun away from her temple. "I can't! I can't!" she whimpered. The officer would remind her of her family members to distract her, but she was confused. "I'll just go ahead and kill myself," she would threaten. Officer Young advised her that that would only serve to destroy her parents.

Yolanda asked to speak to her mother for the last time, to say good-bye and to ask for forgiveness. She made it a condition for giving up the gun. But the officer explained that he was using a radio device that could not accommodate a three-way call. He may have thought it was a trick on Yolanda's part and that once she spoke with her mother she would proceed to blow her brains out. He promised her that if she turned herself in he would put her in touch with her family through a regular phone.

"I'm gonna be exposed to all the friends and the media and I don't … wanna do that … I want you [to] take everybody away from here … Get everybody just to leave. I'm so ashamed!…"

"You can redeem yourself, Yolanda. People do wrong things all the time and their life changes and they start doing things right again."

"I can't because I-I did something so shameful, I-I-I don't deserve to just stay in this world."

The conversation became increasingly painful. The police officer appealed to her faith. "Do you believe in God?"

"I believe in God … I don't think I can forgive myself. God can forgive me. I just wanna dieeeeee…" she wailed. Officer Young asked her to let go of the revolver, and she said she had no intention of harming anyone except herself.

The officer tried to give her support and to win her over with words of affection. "Let me give you my strength now … you must be very tired … baby…" But it was useless.

"…But I have the thing [the hammer] backwards … I am ready to shoot … This is it, Larry! Please forgive me somebody and everybody the trouble [I've caused] your policemen."

"No, Yolanda. Please lay it [the gun] on the floor," he warned her.

Throughout her protests, he continued to repeat the words he had learned during the hostage negotiation training he received through the police department. He promised that the moment she gave herself up he would cover her with a jacket so the television cameras would not be able to view her and that she would be able to speak to her lawyer as soon as she turned herself in. In fact, several times they thought they had her convinced and that she would get out of the truck, but at the last minute she would change her mind or have a panic attack. At one point, she had one foot outside the door but they turned on powerful spotlights to better illuminate the scene and she got scared.

Night had fallen on Corpus Christi; a light rain misted the scene. Officer Isaac Valencia, Larry Young's right-hand man, reached an agreement with Yolanda: If she left the truck at 7 P.M. on the dot, he would make sure that the spotlights were turned off so that no one could see her. Yolanda left the weapon on the seat of the truck and got out. But the special agents on the case threw everything off again. When Yolanda saw they were armed, she felt her terror rising and she jumped back inside once again, repeating over and over: "They're carrying guns! They're carrying guns! They're going to kill me! They're going to kill me!"

I found it curious that someone who up to that moment had threatened to kill herself more than 270 times would be afraid that someone might make her wish come true. But I suppose that only someone who has lived through it can understand that logic, or the lack of it. The fact is that no matter how hard Valencia and Young tried to convince her that the officers were armed as part of their duties and that they were not going to harm her, she did not want to come out again. The game was back to square one.

"I'm hurting real bad … I don't want to live anymore, but I don't know how to pull this trigger."

Once again, Young begged her not to do it and soothed her with words of compassion. Yolanda was exhausted, and her hands were crippling her after all the hours of holding the phone and the gun—her only weapons against the world and herself. She put the revolver down on the seat for a moment, as if she were about to surrender.

But then something unexpected happened. As is common with some cellular phones, her phone picked up interference from local radio signals while she talked with the police. Yolanda heard a broadcaster announce that Selena had died and her desperation increased. Yolanda chastised her "friend Larry" for not having been sincere and for keeping the singer's tragic end from her, especially since earlier she had expressed that she wanted to go see Selena at the hospital. With excuses and justifications, Officer Young tried to explain himself and told her that he simply did not know what was happening at the hospital. And he advised her not to believe everything she heard on the radio.

What little hope she had left vanished. She put the gun up against her temple again. Ironically, the radio station was playing the theme song from the television show, M*A*S*H—the tune called "Suicide Is Painless."

Perhaps that was her most difficult moment. Sometime later, Yolanda spoke, "I want to die after what I've done to my best friend … I'm so sorry … they dragged me into this … God knows how much I tried to help her … She and I kept a good relationship as friends. More than friends. As sisters, as sisters. I have lost the only friend I ever had in my entire life…"

"I know you're hurting…" said Young. "I don't understand why you don't want to live anymore"

"Because the people don't love me no more … they were threatening me."

"Who's threatening you?"

"My friend's father … He threatened to kill me. He slashed two tires in my car. He put two bullets in my car. I had to find … protection for myself. I went to San Antonio to live with my parents. He threatened me over there every single day. He says he doesn't want me next to his daughter."

Yolanda kept telling the officer that she was only trying to help Selena, but that her father had taken it the wrong way. She did not explain what that help consisted of. She told Young that the magnitude of the events before the tragedy was enormous, that she had many stories to reveal, but that she could not. As I heard all this in court, I asked myself, "What is Yolanda referring to?" I had no way of knowing that eventually Yolanda herself would tell me she was referring to "the secret."

Yolanda blamed Abraham for having made her life a living hell and of sexually abusing her. "He stuck a knife in my vagina ... He raped me about a month and a half ago. He told me not to tell anyone or he would kill me ... He raped me in my apartment ... Larry, I don't have proof. I never went to the hospital. I never had anything done because he told me ... 'If you tell anybody ... I will kill your family.' He-he has done other stuff to other people, Larry..."

Now it became clear to us why, on the first day of the trial, Valdez had asked Selena's father during his testimony if he had ever had sexual relations with the accused. He wanted these allegations denied knowing that they would turn up in the tapes later.

On the tape, Young is heard encouraging Yolanda to formally accuse the man she claims violated her, in order to keep her from killing herself. "If you think about hurting yourself, how are we going to be able to do anything about Abraham? ... The only way we can do anything about Abraham is for you to be here ... I wish I'd known about this earlier..."

She responded that in the past she had called the police and her lawyer to report Quintanilla, but no one did anything about it. At one point, she became quite paranoid, looking around and saying, "I know Abraham's around here somewhere to kill me."

Ironically, Abraham was nowhere near her. He had run to be with his wounded and dying daughter. The last thing in the world he cared about was Yolanda's fate. But here and now, in the courtroom, he was indeed just a few steps from her.

Yolanda also told Larry, "This man [Abraham] was so evil to me ... My father even told me. He warned me about that. He said, 'You better get out of there, Yolanda, 'cause this man is gonna trap you...' I never listened to my father ... Look what happened."

Officer Young repeatedly tried to show her that he was on her side and to make another attempt to get her to leave the truck: "We wouldn't let him [Quintanilla] hurt you ... But we can't help you ... if you don't let us ... Come on. Put the gun down."

Yolanda would not obey. Young put Officer Valencia on the line temporarily in the hope that he might succeed. He asked Yolanda what else Abraham had done to her. At that moment, she started to speak in Spanish for the first time and her words came out in spurts, like water under pressure making its way out of the tiny opening that was her mouth. "He led me to this ... He threw me out of the house ... He threw me out of their life ... Selena was hiding me ... She didn't want her father to know."

She claimed Selena had lodged her in a number of motels to prevent Abraham from finding her. She said that in following Selena's instructions, she had stayed at the Bayfront Inn, then the Budget Inn and, finally, the Days Inn. I was surprised at how easily she recalled these places in the midst of her hysteria. If she had invented them, then she was a more than capable liar. As I indicated earlier, when I checked on her statements I found that she had indeed stayed in all these places in the weeks prior to Selena's death. And during this time, she had been seen accompanying the singer on more than one occasion.

Five of the nine hours of the siege were recorded on tape and were played in court from beginning to end, over the course of that Monday and into Tuesday. After several hours of negotiations, an interesting event took place: In their eagerness to get her to surrender, Officers Young and Valencia told Yolanda to be careful with the weapon as it was defective and could go off by itself.

At that moment, we heard for the first time what had happened in room 158 according to Yolanda. "I brought this gun to kill myself, not her, and she told me, 'Yolanda, I don't want you to kill yourself.' And we were talking about that when I took it out and pointed it to my head, and when I pointed it to my head, she opened the door. I said, 'Selena, close that door,' and when I did that the gun went off." When she finished speaking, Valencia told her, "It sounds to me like there was an accident."

The prosecution states that with those comments the officers unknowingly planted an idea in the suspect's head. They gave her an out since several times after that she repeated that it had all been an accident. But the defense maintained that although Yolanda had not used the word "accident" previously, she had said from the very beginning that she had no intention of harming Selena and that she had never aimed the gun at her. I watched the accused listen to her own words, hanging her head. As her taped voice reverberated around the courtroom, tears ran down her cheeks, one by one. Much later when I asked her if she was crying for herself, she said that she had been crying for the singer. But I suspect she was crying for both herself and Selena.

At another point on the tape, Yolanda asked Officer Young to pray with her. And they did. Later on she expressed her concern about Selena's family and how they must be suffering. She said that she included Abraham in her thoughts, no matter what he had done to her, for he was still a human being.

Young, who possessed an almost saintly patience, explained to her how easy it would be to surrender. All she had to do was let go of the gun and open the door. He would join her to cover her face with a jacket to prevent the photographers from taking their pictures, and he would get her out of there. She agreed, without realizing that in order to make the long walk to the truck, Young would no longer be able to communicate with her on the cell phone. As soon as she lost contact with him, she lost all faith and started to scream uncontrollably: "Where's Larry? Where is Larry?" The frightened shrieking echoed against the courtroom walls: "Larryyyyyyyyyyyy!" Yolanda would not stop pleading for him, and in the courtroom, those minutes seemed like an eternity as we listened to her ask for him over and over again. Her voice was filled with such desperation that her anguish lodged in the hearts of many who heard her on the tape inside the courtroom. Valencia tried to explain to her what was happening, but it was not until Young turned back and picked up his radio that she calmed down somewhat.

At 9:30 P.M., after several other attempts, Yolanda finally, peacefully turned herself in to the authorities. She was taken to police headquarters. The drama at the Days Inn had come to an end.

After hearing her endless shrieks and wails, her plea for Larry became a joke among the journalists and reporters. Whenever a member of the press was looking for a colleague outside the courthouse, they would scream jokingly, "Where's Larrryyy?" Even Larry himself was surprised at his sudden fame. Overnight, the phrase would become commercially viable. By the next morning, T-shirts and buttons went on sale. They all said WHERE'S LARRY?

In court, Mark Skurka called John Houston, another officer who had been present at the siege, to testify. He described how he saw Yolanda point the revolver at her head as she spoke on the cell phone. Skurka abruptly interrupted him and asked, "And how many times did the gun go off while Yolanda was doing all this?"

"None," answered the officer.

Without question, a most effective blow.

As it turns out, the first four hours of negotiations were never taped. The official story is that they were not recorded because during that time the police were mobilizing their forces to cover the scene at the Days Inn and it took a considerable amount of time to set up the sophisticated radio system required to tape the conversations. But Arnold

García told me that perhaps segments of the tapes were erased, or even that the tapes themselves disappeared, since during those moments Yolanda may have touched upon delicate topics.

It's highly unlikely that there was a conspiracy here, but I'm convinced that in those missing hours there were, in fact, sensitive details that did not come out during or after the trial. One day when I found myself submerged in the swamp of court documents, I stumbled upon an interesting note. It was one of the small scraps of paper that the police officers passed to one another to communicate while they were negotiating for Yolanda's surrender. Law-enforcement agents tend to use this method in this type of situation to avoid interrupting communication with those under siege or in a hostage situation, to avoid appearing indecisive or to communicate to each other the line of questioning being followed or topics they want to focus on.

On the piece of paper was the word "ABORTION" in capital letters. I did not know in what context it had been mentioned. Months after the trial I called Officer Young at home and asked him about the note. He spoke to me about what he had discussed with the suspect before the tape recorder had been turned on. At that time, Yolanda told him she had been sexually abused not once, but two times, and that after the first instance she had to end a pregnancy. He himself admitted that during those first hours that were never recorded everything was quite confusing. But he said he was certain that Yolanda did not know Selena was mortally wounded. She asked him several times if the singer was going to return to the motel. I used that opportunity to ask him, "Larry, what do you think really happened?" He answered me without hesitation. "It was not a premeditated murder," he said. "She pulled the trigger in a moment of panic, but not necessarily to kill her."

Someone else who believed Yolanda's words was a psychiatrist we contacted for *Primer Impacto*. Our expert on the mysterious workings of the mind listened to the tapes and maintained, on our program, that it would be very difficult for anyone to be able to lie so consistently in a situation like the siege, one full of surprises and tremendous tension. Yolanda had not had time to rehearse her story and it was obvious that she was tortured by something. According to his diagnosis, which was very general since he had only a limited amount of airtime to analyze the tapes, the voice is desperate and anguished, but coherent.

The tapes were a blessing for the defense. On them Yolanda presented her side of the story without being on the witness stand, where she would have been exposed to interrogation by the prosecution. But what is crucial about them is that they make Yolanda Saldívar a human being. Hearing her crying, screaming, asking for God's mercy, praying and showing her remorse made it very difficult not to feel for her. For a short period, the accused ceased to be a monster and became a feeling and hurting woman. Afterward, we interviewed several members of the public who had been in court, and to our surprise most of them felt sympathy for her.

On our show Tuesday evening, our legal advisers differed in their opinions. Castillo maintained that Yolanda's claim that Abraham had sexually violated her should be investigated. Rangel said the opposite: "These are only allegations. There's no proof of any kind." We went back and forth on the case, but no matter how much we speculated, it was impossible to know what was going through the minds of the twelve people who held Yolanda's future in their hands.

On the streets, everyone had an opinion about the accused. One group set up a sidewalk game using a photo of Yolanda's face as a target; the goal was to land a dart on her nose. Each time someone hit a bull's-eye, they would all yell mockingly, "Oh, it was an accident!"

On the following day, Wednesday the eighteenth, the prosecution called on Robert Garza, the Texas Ranger who'd observed Yolanda's confession. Valdez wanted to stay ahead of the defense and neutralize the testimony in advance. But this didn't happen. Garza verified, just as he had during the preliminary hearings in Corpus, that he had seen Yolanda making gestures to explain her intention to kill herself, and he claimed to have heard her say that it had all been an accident. These statements took the edge off Yolanda's confession, which Valdez was using as a sharpened weapon against the defense.

Then it was Paul Rivera's turn to testify. Valdez reviewed with the officer every single phase of Yolanda's interrogation to show that it had been carried out according to regulations.

When Tinker approached the witness stand to cross-examine Officer Rivera, few people could imagine what a difficult moment it was for both of them. I knew their friendship had lasted for years and that because of all the tension from the Corpus Christi hearings they barely spoke to each other, for obvious reasons. During his questioning, Tinker repeated some of the same arguments he had used in Corpus Christi to expose the officer's potential conflict of interests and to show that he could not be objective about Yolanda. He recalled that Rivera had a poster of Selena in his office and that his brother had been Abraham Quintanilla's army buddy. But this time, as far as Rivera was concerned, Tinker really twisted the knife. The defense attorney revealed that the detective had had the bad taste to bring him a Selena T-shirt, a present to Tinker from Abraham Quintanilla, sent to butter him up.

When I spoke with Rivera nearly a year after the trial, he told me that what Tinker had done had hurt him deeply. He said that when he brought Tinker the T-shirt, he'd had friendly intentions, and he felt that this well-intentioned gesture had been used against him. He sounded sincere, though apparently there were no lasting hard feelings. When I asked him how things stood between him and Tinker at this point, he said, "Great! Last Christmas he sent me a bottle of whiskey as a present. We're still friends, just like before … I just finished testifying in a case in favor of one of Tinker's clients." The detective laughed. I guess that's the way it is among law enforcement professionals who are often on opposite sides of the courtroom—sometimes they love each other, sometimes they would rather see each other dead.

I suspect that that Wednesday in October was one day when Rivera would rather have seen Tinker six feet under. With skillfull questioning, the defense attorney showed that Yolanda signed the confession after being pressured by

Rivera in a variety of ways; namely, that she was exhausted after eleven hours without a sip of water, eating, sleeping or going to the bathroom—all this after the traumatic experience of holing up in the truck with the gun. In the same fashion, Tinker asked the officer why they had not allowed his client to see her family until after she had signed the confession. Paul Rivera did not provide many convincing answers.

Tinker also questioned why they had not recorded Yolanda's interrogation and why Rivera had destroyed the notes he had taken during that time. Even more significant, why had the police failed to provide a lawyer when the law requires it, despite the fact that on the tapes made during the standoff in the truck, law-enforcement agents could clearly be heard offering Yolanda legal assistance in exchange for her surrender? The defense left the impression that the police had something to hide.

Surprisingly, the trial was taking a slight turn in favor of the defendant. The tapes made her a real-life human being and presented her version of the events in an uncorrupted manner. And the questionable way in which the police had behaved did not help the prosecution either. People on the street who wanted to see her convicted started to worry. Even one of the courtroom guards told me quietly that after seeing the evidence, he thought the suspect was innocent. Were the jurors thinking the same thing? Tinker was efficiently cobbling together the theory of a conspiracy on the part of the police.

Rangel gave his perspective on the turn of events: "This attack on the police is one of Tinker's tactics to get the attention off the accused. In a very able manner, the defense has transformed Saldívar from aggressor to victim of the police officers. This should have been a good day for the prosecution, but it did not turn out well, since now we don't know if the confession signed by the accused carries as much weight as before."

In Castillo's opinion, there was still something amiss. According to him, it was obvious that the police were collaborating with the prosecution and did not want to answer questions from the defense. He agreed with Rangel that Yolanda's role had become that of victim and added his point of view: "The way the police handled matters does not look good. There were many procedural errors. Something smells rotten." Regarding Paul Rivera he added, "He thought that as well as being a police officer he was also Yolanda's judge and jury, because he convicted her as guilty from the first moment. That's why he ignored her rights."

Both attorneys agreed that the trial, with all its twists and turns, was like a roller coaster.

Oddly enough, it was after this, which had been unquestionably the defense's best day, that the Mexican Mafia, one of the most powerful prison gangs in the United States, made its presence felt. During a press conference after court, Tinker mentioned he had received in the mail a postcard signed by the gang, threatening him and his family. It was never made clear why the Mexican Mafia planned to off Tinker, but I imagine that among the gang members there must be quite a few Selena fans. What I do not understand is why the gang then threatened the prosecution. Valdez says he received a similar missive from the same group although he, too, refused to elaborate. He did comment on the threats made against his rival Tinker. "Yolanda has the right to be represented by a good lawyer … and she has one." And although both sides made it clear to the public that enduring threats was part of the job, I know that in private, behind closed doors, they were worried and took the threats quite seriously.

Univisión's mobile studio, set up on the street next to the courthouse, was next to the one belonging to *Ocurrió Así,* the show produced by Telemundo that is broadcast at the same time as *Primer Impacto.* The only thing that separated us was a piece of canvas through which I could hear almost everything they said and vice versa. At one point, between commercials, I heard their anchor Enrique Gratas offer vague commentary to viewers like "Tomorrow the prosecution will bring out several witnesses, although we don't know how many." When our commercial break was over, I'd go back on air and fill in the blanks since I practically had more information than I needed. "Tomorrow the prosecution plans to present five witnesses, which include the forensic specialist and personnel from the hospital where the singer died." My entire team shared this competitive spirit, and we would laugh when we would hear shrieks from the other side as our competitors listened to what we had done. Eventually, I met Enrique Gratas in person. Though we work in the same business and have comparable positions, we'd never been introduced. One day, I had cigarettes and no matches; he had matches and no cigarettes. We had a brief but pleasant conversation and after our last drags on our cigarettes we went back to the reality of our work.

On the ninth day of the judicial process, the prosecution produced some dramatic but solid testimony that would impress the jury. The testimony on Thursday, October 19, revolved around the different medical opinions regarding Selena's last moments of life.

Louis Elkins, the surgeon who had attended her in the emergency room along with Dr. Vicente Juan, said that when she arrived, Selena was clinically dead. "There was no evidence of neurological function, there was no blood flowing to the brain, her pupils were fixed and dilated. She was not breathing on her own. She had no vital signs." The details that followed were powerfully affecting, if hard to listen to; Selena's right lung was destroyed and her veins were practically empty. The doctors opened her chest in a desperate effort to save her life, but even the transfusions were in vain. In a final attempt they took her into the operating room.

When the doctor was asked if Abraham had ordered him to stop the transfusions for religious reasons, he said he had no knowledge of that request. He explained that she was given transfusions constantly, and that the only person who could have stopped him would have been Selena herself, and she was unconscious the entire time. He made it clear that all the blood in the world would not have brought the singer back to life.

Medical records indicate that Selena's father had indeed requested that the doctors not administer blood because it went against the beliefs of the Jehovah's Witnesses, which the Quintanilla family subscribed to. This request apparently never reached Dr. Elkin's ears.

During the cross-examination, the defense questioned why Abraham was making decisions affecting the well-being of Selena when, by law, that responsibility belonged to her husband, Chris. It seemed like a low blow, and I'm certain it had a negative effect on the jurors. No one is going to pass judgment on a father whose daughter is dying or on the religious beliefs of a family in the midst of crisis.

That same day the graphic photos from the autopsy were brought out. Selena did not seem to be dead, merely asleep. Her body was intact, perfect. The only detail that seemed incongruous was a tiny hole in her back—the bullet's point of entry. Out of respect for her family on my show that afternoon, I did not go into the gruesome details the forensic doctor had revealed as part of his duties. And I won't go into them now. I will tell you that although Lloyd White, the physician, made great efforts to present his findings in a professional and unemotional way, nearly everyone in the courtroom was affected. One jury member could not contain herself and burst into tears, bringing everything to a halt until a tissue could be found for her to compose herself and dry her tears. Yolanda Saldívar remained impassive, her head lowered, as she did for much of the trial. Now we could all see the tangible consequences of the crime. Death was no longer an abstract concept.

The doctor's report indicated that Selena was not pregnant at the time of death, as was later erroneously reported by a magazine. The report also made it clear that there were no traces of drugs or alcohol in her body. The official cause of death is that she bled to death. After concluding his report, the forensic expert announced his firm conclusion: "This was a homicide, not an accident."

The prosecution also called on a firearms examiner and weapons expert for the police department. After examining the revolver that had been used in the killing, Ed Mckinstry concluded that it was not defective. During cross, the defense asked if a person unfamiliar with weapons could accidentally pull the trigger. "I suppose so," answered the expert, "although it seems very difficult to me." He added that the hard part lies in the fact that in order to fire a .38, the person pulling the trigger must use a great amount of pressure. The mechanism requires a conscious human action before a bullet is released.

Though the defense was able to prove that, as a precaution, the same weapons expert keeps his own firearms in the trunk of his vehicle for fear that they might go off accidentally, the damage was done. The defense's theory of an accidental gunshot was not technically possible.

Valdez presented photographs of the trail of blood Selena had left between room 158 and the motel's reception area—the path by which her life was leaving her, step by step. The red drops covered a distance of more than 390 feet. One juror's eyes widened dramatically at the sight. We also saw graphic photos of the room after the crime. Valdez pointed out that there were obvious blood stains on the door, indicating that it was impossible for Yolanda not to know her friend had been wounded. This meant that she had not come to her aid because she chose not to.

After several days and thirty-three witnesses, the prosecution finished presenting its case. It had been a bad day for the defense. Rangel summed it up astutely: "Today, the principal witness was Selena herself. Her presence was felt; she told us what took place with her body, her blood; she told us everything without saying a word."

Meanwhile out on the streets, the groups of people waiting for news grew larger and larger. They closely followed the proceedings, calling for justice. A street gang paraded Yolanda's coffin on the sidewalks, drawing applause from the crowd. They wanted to see her dead.

Friday marked the end of the second week of the trial and the beginning of the defense's arguments. We all expected a long parade of defense witnesses like that of the prosecution, but once again Tinker surprised us. In just three hours, the old poker player made his case with only five witnesses and one wild card.

The principal strategy was to discredit the testimony of the prosecution's witnesses. Tinker recalled Ruben De León to clarify certain details. The witness declared that the door to the reception area was never locked; Shawna Vela implied that this had been done at Selena's request, because of her fear that Yolanda would shoot her again. De León remembered that a police officer was able to enter the lobby area at one point precisely because the door was not locked.

Barbara Shultz took her turn on the stand. Tinker, in an effort to show his client's credibility, asked her who she was married to; Shultz answered that her husband was a Corpus Christi police officer. She managed to unravel Shawna Vela's testimony. Shultz also had been in the motel's reception area when Selena, mortally wounded, ran in. But in Shultz's version, Selena never asked that the door be locked. In fact, Selena never said a word. She just moaned. The motel manager said that Shawna, her former employee, was not trustworthy.

Shultz's main contribution to the defense's case was to suggest that the witnesses had "contaminated" one another's testimony—an idea that Tinker had mentioned several times. She said that all the employees who were called to testify by the prosecution had gathered together shortly after Selena's death and had shared their versions of events, reaching a consensus as to what had happened. Using Shultz, Tinker managed to cast doubt on the legitimacy of the testimony of the prosecution witnesses. Now it seemed believable that they had all gotten together and agreed on what they should say.

For the first time another cleaning woman from the motel gave her testimony. Gloria Magaña also made the words of the prosecution's star witnesses appear doubtful. In her version, neither Trinidad Espinoza nor Norma Marie Martínez was able to see Yolanda's alleged chase after Selena, because the singer was simply not in their line of sight. Magaña was. She claimed to have seen Selena running through the parking lot, but she never saw Yolanda. Gloria was not present when the other employees supposedly gathered together to discuss their versions.

Tinker called Detective Paul Rivera to the stand. During the brief exchange, the officer admitted that for months he had known about the existence of the tapes made during Yolanda's siege, but he had not notified the defense about them. (Ordinarily, law enforcement officers are required to disclose such potential evidence to the

court.) Tinker successfully left the impression that the officer did not want the defense team to have access to the
tapes because they would favor his client.

Now Tinker needed to nail down his hypothesis that
Abraham Quintanilla had been a dominating father who
smothered his daughter with unrelenting control. He called
on Marilyn Greer, Selena's seventh-grade teacher. At first
Quintanilla did not recognize her since he had not seen her
in over a decade. But in the blink of an eye, her testimony
refreshed his memory. Greer declared that Selena had been
a brilliant young woman, with the potential for graduating
with honors and easily obtaining a college scholarship. But
her talent was being wasted. While other girls did what was
appropriate for their age, Selena was forced to travel the
state, singing at parties, bars and other nightspots until
dawn. She was exposed to an environment that was not at
all healthy for a young woman of thirteen. Greer is the
teacher who had argued with Quintanilla ten years earlier
and had threatened to report him to the authorities.
Eventually, Abraham took his daughter out of school and
made her finish her studies via correspondence school. All
this emerged in her testimony.

With Marylin Greer, the defense completed its presentation of witnesses. No one imagined that Tinker would
choose not to call Abraham Quintanilla to the stand.

But the biggest surprise came next. Tinker was playing
for the highest stakes, putting all his bets on one number.
He asked the court that his client's innocence or guilt be
judged on one charge only: first-degree murder. Westergren, who would make the final ruling on Tinker's

request, had the option of giving the jurors instructions to consider other charges, such as murder in the second degree or negligent criminal homicide, which carried lesser penalties than first-degree murder. But Tinker seemed convinced that the jury would be forced to acquit his client; he did not believe that the prosecution had proved beyond a reasonable doubt that Yolanda fired the gun with premeditated intention—a requirement for her to be convicted of first-degree murder. He was placing all his eggs in one basket, and more than one jaw dropped when the judge accepted Tinker's proposal.

It was then that the Saldívar family let their feelings out, giving vent to emotion they had been storing up for weeks. They left the courtroom embracing one another, their faces red from all the crying, giving one another whatever consolation they could. I found out that they had gone directly to church from the courtroom to pray for their beloved family member. All that was left now was to hear the closing arguments from both sides and await the verdict. It was an anguish-filled waiting period.

To pass the time, all the nicotine addicts—myself included—dashed out to a small balcony where we were allowed to smoke, as we had done during the recesses between sessions. Fortunately, as bad a habit as smoking is, it came in handy during the trial. (I've since quit!) I was the only journalist to use the balcony but I would always find Valdez, Arnold García and, on occasion, Paul Rivera there. Even key witnesses took their turn out there. It was during these breaks that I obtained anecdotes and details for my coverage. The smokers regularly opened their mouths to exhale—and to reveal information. Awaiting closing arguments, no one said much. They were all in shock.

That afternoon, yet another surprise took place. In a secretive fashion, Arnold García approached me and in a whisper asked, "Do you want to have lunch with Tinker and me?" This was incredible to me. Not only because it was actually happening, but also because it was Tinker, the very same person who had hung up on me months earlier, who was now inviting me.

The strategy for this lunch could have been borrowed from a spy movie. A few moments before we were to leave, Arnold García came by my trailer to tell me where we were to meet. "I'll wait for you at the corner," he said, in a sneaky tone reminiscent of a teenage boyfriend.

At the corner a huge car was waiting. A door opened quickly as I approached, and was closed with equal speed as soon as I entered. We drove to a Mexican restaurant. It was quite hectic and full of people. As we walked in Tinker looked seriously at a group of three beautiful blond women and said to me, "How much do you want to bet that I'm going to kiss one of those three beauties?" Before giving me time to answer, he walked up to one of them, grabbed her and planted a passionate kiss on her lips. I was astounded. Fortunately it turned out to be his wife who was waiting for him, along with their nieces. That, I discovered, is Tinker's sense of humor.

I expected that something extraordinary would come out of this encounter—an exclusive, an interesting fact at the very least—so I was very careful in our conversation. So careful that by the end of the meal, although it may seem unbelievable, we hadn't talked about the trial! The conversation centered on Mexican food and the one passion Tinker and I have in common: animals. Throughout the entire lunch we spoke about our pet dogs. At the very end, though, and with emotion, Tinker told me that my hard work and objectivity had restored his faith in the media. Coming from this particular source, these words truly gave me reason to be proud. I was glad and honored to have earned his respect.

I was able to obtain something new out of this lunch after all. As the conversation meandered from one topic to another, I quietly asked Arnold about the mysterious suitcase that Selena had taken to the Days Inn. It was full of clothing as though she were about to go off on a trip. "You're not going to believe me," said Arnold smiling, "but at this very moment the suitcase is in the trunk of Tinker's car." I never saw it, but he insisted it was true. So the suitcase was not with the police. Instead, some twist of fate had landed the suitcase in the trunk of a car belonging to the lawyer defending the woman accused of murdering its owner. It occurred to me: If people pay thousands of dollars for an item of Elvis's clothing, what price wouldn't the fans pay for the personal belongings of this new legend? And there they were, baking in the trunk of a car when perhaps they should have been in a museum.

Later I found out that it was a large, black leather suitcase on rollers, and that there was a name on it: Chris Pérez. Inside there was enough clothing for several days, including underclothing, boots and the black jacket the singer had worn while taping a music video with the Barrio Boyzz.

What did Selena want it for? She did not have any trip officially scheduled, nor any concert planned. Was it for another secret trip to Monterrey? Or perhaps a more decisive departure, since she also had a permit to work in Mexico? Of course, she never reached her final destination. Months later I learned that the suitcase had landed in the Saldívars' home. They still have it.

That afternoon María Elida called me in our production trailer. She was very worried. Neither she nor her parents had clearly understood the card Tinker had played in court, nor the consequences it might have on Yolanda's fate. Since they had no way to get in touch with him, they asked me. They were desperate. I did my best to explain Tinker's legal strategy, but finally I put Castillo, one of our legal experts, on the line. He rapidly cleared up their doubts and fears. When I had the receiver back in my hands, something totally unexpected happened.

"I have a surprise for you, María," said María Elida confidently. "There are three of us on the line, not two!"

"What?" I asked her without quite understanding what was happening.

"Yes, we're on a conference call," she answered. And then she added the introduction: "Go ahead, Yoli," she said, laughing.

"Hi, María. How are you?"

It was Yolanda. Her voice sounded sweet, almost childlike, so different from the scream on the tapes. I was struck dumb, but I composed myself and said hello, as if I knew her. We were both nervous. She was not supposed to be speaking to anyone, much less someone from the media.

In a totally convincing tone, she told me, "Thank you for treating my family with decency. When I get out of here, no matter what happens, whether it's in a house or in jail, I'm going to speak only with one person and that person is going to be you. But I'm never going to tell *what happened in that room* to anyone, never. I know my daughter in heaven is grateful to me for that; I know she wants it to be that way." She repeated that last phrase as though she were talking to herself. What was the mystery? Why keep quiet at this point?

Yolanda then lowered her voice and asked me as though consulting an oracle, "What do you think the verdict is going to be?" I kept quiet for an instant to think through my response and its consequences. I answered her ambiguously, but sincerely. "Anything could happen. You have to be ready for anything. But the outcome and the place won't matter. I'll be fair to you in my interview."

We hung up. When he saw the cat-who-just-ate-the-canary look on my face, my technical director asked me, "Who were you talking to?"

"No one important," I answered, smiling inside.

I felt satisfied. My politics of respect had paid off—not only with professional results, but also because personally, I felt I'd done the right thing and had treated Yolanda with fairness. Feeling energized by my conversation, I went to touch up my makeup. By this point, the bags under my eyes required twice as much.

That evening on *Primer Impacto,* our famous astrologer, Walter Mercado, read the astral cards corresponding to Yolanda and Selena. From the very beginning, he said, the stars forecasted a tragic end for both if their paths ever crossed. The zodiac predicted a short life for the singer. She would come and go quickly like a shooting star. Walter also described a vision he had about Selena and explained that in it, the singer "forgave" Yolanda. A viewer came by a bit later, very serious, and asked me, "María Celeste, in that message Selena sent, did she explain if she forgave Yolanda for murder or for letting the gun go off by accident?" Great question. Every time I think of it I laugh out loud. Unfortunately, Walter's mystic moment was not long enough to clear up what we all wanted to know. I also found out that Yolanda had seen Walter's segment in her cell and was not at all pleased.

I returned to Miami just for the weekend because I wanted to connect with my loved ones again, with my usual life, and try to remember who I was. The trial was consuming me and kept me from focusing on personal things. It was useless. I couldn't do it. My thoughts were constantly on what was going to happen during the coming week when we thought the verdict would be announced. On top of that, I spent Saturday and Sunday calling Monterrey, trying to get an interview with Dr. Martínez and landing an exclusive as soon as possible. I knew he had a lot to say and that his lawyer had not hinted again that he wanted money in exchange for an interview. Finally, the doctor agreed to talk on *Primer Impacto* on the condition that his legal counsel was present. It was a reasonable request and the interview was scheduled for a few days later.

On Monday, October 23, the trial entered its third week and the defense presented their closing arguments. Fred Hagans argued that the accident version of the story had been suppressed. He also recalled the way Officer Rivera had handled the interrogation: "He wasn't interested in pursuing justice. He was interested in making a case. He knew in the early hours that this was a big case. He wanted to be the one to get Yolanda." Later he said, "There's an old saying that if you can't trust the messenger, you can't trust the message … You can't trust Paul Rivera."

Hagans added that Selena took the time on March 31 to take Yolanda to the hospital, even though she had a recording session that day, because she still considered Yolanda to be a dear friend. He recalled what one of the gun store employees had said: that a revolver with the hammer cocked back could be fired by just using one's little finger. Hagans lambasted the prosecution for showing photos of Selena in the morgue and the trail of blood at the motel. He called it a sensationalistic move whose only purpose was to manipulate the jury's emotions. He closed by asking the jury to avoid being turned into a tool of vengeance for a rabid father. "We're not here to satisfy the vengeance of an angry man."

Tinker followed with additional closing arguments for the defense. From the beginning he appeared to be rambling. Usually, Tinker can give commanding speeches without using notes or other cues, but on this occasion his thinking did not seem organized. He left questions unanswered and failed to tie up loose ends in his client's version of events. He himself recognized his lack of coherence when he asked the jury to excuse him for jumping from one topic to another. He covered himself by saying that his mind worked like a pinball machine.

Tinker asked the jury several questions: Why was no proof of Yolanda's theft presented? Why didn't the prosecution ask the accountants to testify? Why were the fan club files never presented? He finished his argument by asking the jury not to fear the public's reaction should they deliver an unpopular verdict. He closed with the following words, his eyes fixed on the doors to the courtroom: "If Selena were present, she would come in [through those doors], and with her usual smile, she would forgive Yolanda. She herself would tell you that everything had been a fatal accident." The defense attorney did not imagine that Valdez, the prosecutor, would appropriate that phrase in a few minutes and include it in his speech, turning it around to close his argument with even greater dramatic impact.

The prosecution opened their closing arguments most effectively. First came Skurka, who, in my opinion, stole the show. He started by displaying a large photo of Selena next to the jury panel and saying that Selena had been reduced to a mere picture thanks to the March 31 actions of the defendant. Somehow the photo made it seem as if the dead singer were there in person. A radio reporter next to me confided in me solemnly, "This is giving me goose bumps."

Skurka explained that since there had been no witness in room 158, Yolanda should be judged on the way she acted before and after the gun went off. "If you'll notice, you'll see that her actions are consistent with those of a murderer," he stated firmly. Then he, too, fired off a barrage of questions that had not been answered: "Why did she give different reasons for having purchased the gun? Why did Yolanda Saldívar hold on to the gun in her hand if she knew it had gone off accidentally? Why, if she had been a nurse and knew how to administer first aid, did she not help the wounded victim? Why didn't she call 911? ... Use your logic," he suggested to the members of the jury.

While Selena had left her mark on the world of music, Skurka stated, Yolanda Saldívar cowardly left her mark on Selena's back. Skurka methodically attempted to erode Yolanda's credibility. Placing a white presentation board on an easel, the attorney—who seemed to be a master at using props in the courtroom—made marks to keep count of each contradiction in Yolanda's version of events. He reminded everyone that she had offered three different excuses for purchasing the weapon: First, she said she needed the revolver to defend herself against one of her patient's relatives; second, she said it was to protect herself against Abraham Quintanilla; and last, she wanted the gun to do away with herself. Skurka said that the same thing had occurred with Yolanda's tale of her rape. The assailant had been a mysterious man, but according to the tapes she had also been violated in her apartment by Selena's father. When he finished, the board was covered with marks, as if he'd been keeping score. It was a powerful visual aid.

The prosecutor pointed out that if Yolanda was going to kill herself on March 31, she had ample time to do so; that someone who is going to commit suicide does not have extra bullets in her purse, like Yolanda had. He questioned that if it really had been an accident, why did she not say the word "accident" until five hours into the standoff? Skurka categorized the accident version as hogwash.

In his final comments, Skurka said that the defense had used the same strategy that a squid uses—when they saw the prosecution launch its attack, they spewed ink to prevent anyone from seeing clearly. The defense was blaming everyone else, inventing a conspiracy to take attention off the accused. Skurka asked the jury not to fall into their trap, to concentrate on the evidence and to remember the final words of the forensic doctor: Selena's death had not been an accident. It had been a homicide.

Carlos Valdez continued the prosecution's argument. But before saying a word, he made a reverential gesture toward Selena's portrait, as though she were the Blessed Virgin. Then he made a direct appeal to the jurors' common sense: "They [the defense] say it was an accident, although everything points in the other direction."

Valdez brought out a large calendar for the month of March and used it to point out the chronological order of events that, according to him, had caused Yolanda to commit the crime. When he reached the fateful date of March 31, the prosecutor said that "as Selena walked out the door … everything she [Saldívar] had in her life, everything that she is in this life, was walking out the door and she wasn't going to let it happen."

According to the prosecutor, Yolanda hated the singer's father and that is why she sought to do him harm. "And how do you hurt Abraham Quintanilla? You shoot his daughter. A diabolical mind will shoot the person he loves the most." Valdez appeared organized and his thinking was quite logical.

Finally, the prosecutor referred to Tinker's final words. He reminded everyone that if Selena were still alive, there would be no reason for a trial. She could not walk through the door and lighten the hearts of those present with her smile because Yolanda had killed her. At the same time he said this, the prosecutor pointed to Yolanda with an accusatory finger. But even after he finished his sentence he kept his finger pointed at her for a few seconds longer. It was a highly charged moment.

With these last words echoing in their minds, the jury retired to deliberate. It was the beginning of the end.

On the street we were all on hold, waiting for the decisive moment. In the trailer we would drink cup after cup of coffee. Rangel and Castillo were at my side constantly during that tense period. Two hours and twenty minutes later we heard the announcement that the jury had reached a verdict and that it would be announced in a matter of minutes. I dropped everything and ran from the trailer to our street studio, where we were prepared to go live. The quick run had left me disheveled; my hair was like Medusa's and I found myself so out of breath that when I was given my cue I didn't know how I managed to speak. And they say television is a glamorous field! I told viewers that in a matter of seconds we would hear the verdict.

As the camera rolled, I hooked up my IFB and heard the sounds of the courtroom. Judge Westergren's voice came through as clear as a bell. He began by asking the jury if they had reached a verdict. Then he asked all present to contain their reactions once the verdict was read. On the street, thousands had gathered in front of the building. In silence they waited for the results.

With a firm voice Judge Westergren read the decision: Yolanda Saldívar was guilty of first-degree murder.

As I listened to it in English, I translated simultaneously into Spanish for our viewers. People on the street learned the jury's decision from the reporters and word spread through the crowd like wildfire. Some yelled in delight, others cried with emotion and still others knelt and prayed. For them justice had been done. People came from all parts of the city, flooding the area around the courthouse, and traffic came to a standstill as a spontaneous street festival suddenly came to life. People danced to Selena's music as it exploded from huge boom boxes. Nothing like this had ever been seen in Houston.

Castillo, who had been in the courtroom during the reading of the verdict, had not missed a single detail. He left the courtroom and ran to our street studio to tell our viewers what he had seen. He described how before hearing the verdict, Yolanda had been hyperventilating and that once she was pronounced guilty, she leaned forward as if she were in pain and began to sob. Her family burst into tears. The Quintanillas kept their composure and were quickly escorted from the courtroom through a side door.

Selena's family descended to the building's basement where a van with tinted windows whisked them from the courthouse; no one saw them leave. The Saldívars had to leave through the main entrance and face the riotous crowd that celebrated their daughter's disgrace even as they yelled, "Now let's kill the murderer!" They were treated no more humanely than attractions at a carnival. On the way to their car, they were met by a woman whose T-shirt read, in

Spanish, YOLANDA SALDIVAR LLORABA SALIVA, a pun on Yolanda's name that roughly translates to "Yolanda Saldívar Cries Tears of Spit." It was a pathetic show. Both families deserved respect.

Rangel and Castillo concluded that the closing arguments had been pivotal to the outcome of the verdict. I could not have agreed more—when I heard Skurka's speech, I knew Yolanda's fate was sealed. The prosecution, with logic and simplicity, had successfully spun their arguments into a tightly woven cloth that they sold to the jurors. On the other hand, the defense began with a promise of fireworks and amazing surprises, but they didn't come through with a memorable show.

Tinker had started the case aggressively and efficiently, yet he and his team seemed to have lost steam by the end. Rangel had commented that, as a judge, he'd never met a more effective defense attorney than Tinker. But that afternoon, he reported that the Tinker he'd seen that morning during the closing arguments was not the man he knew. What had gone wrong for the defense? Did Tinker perhaps begin to think his was a lost cause? Did Yolanda, in an effort to avoid betraying Selena's trust, prevent Tinker from revealing secrets that might have helped her case? Or was it that Tinker did not want to reveal secrets that would have reflected badly on Selena's image? The last thing Tinker needed was for the jury to think of Yolanda as bent on revenge and therefore capable of twisting—or even inventing—information that would set her free. Had Tinker toned down his approach after he received the death threats? After the trial, the attorney would tell Joe Nick Patoski, the *Texas*

Monthly reporter who covered the trial and later wrote a book on Selena, that at least his client's conviction had reduced the chances that someone might kill him. He said it in jest, but in light of the threats, no doubt Tinker was relieved when the show was over.

During a press conference, Valdez said that the verdict did not surprise him; from the very beginning, he knew that it was a simple case of murder. As we listened to him speak, Rangel reminded me that this victory was special for the prosecutor since he had grown up in Selena's neighborhood and he had made a promise to himself to bring about the conviction of the singer's killer. For Valdez and for many others, good had triumphed over evil.

Tinker did not speak to the media after the verdict. I saw him leave through a back door, looking defeated, running away from the tumult and probably in search of solitude. I met up with Arnold García who told me, "We didn't read the jury well."

I wondered in the middle of all this how Yolanda was doing. Before long, I would have my answer.

The following morning Yolanda rang me on the phone. It was a very difficult moment. I almost could not understand her. Between sobs and lamentations, she assured me that the verdict had been unfair, that she was "going to rot in jail" and that she knew she would receive the maximum penalty. She yelled at me over and over again, "María, I am not a cold-blooded murderer!" I was speechless. The only thing I could think to tell her was that she had to prepare herself for the worst and to stay strong for the good of her parents.

During this phone call, in a moment of total desperation, she began to reveal the "truth"—which she had sworn never to speak of—or what she called "Selena's secret" from that moment on. Just like on the Days Inn tapes, her voice changed dramatically and her words began to flow like a wild river. I did not try to get any information out of her. I did not want to take advantage of her in her moment of weakness. It would have been unfair because even though she had not said so, I knew she was calling on me as just another person to whom she could vent her feelings, not because I was a journalist. I was well aware that a jury of her peers had pronounced her a murderer. But now I could only feel compassion for her and her family. She continued to reveal information with the speed and precision of an expert dart player. I asked her no questions, nor did I judge whether the surprising revelations were true or false. The only decent thing to do was simply to listen. I knew the day would come when I would be able to question her in front of a TV camera, when we would be on equal footing. But now the situation and my attitude were quite different.

After the anguished phone conversation ended, I turned to the day's newspapers. The front-page headline of The *Houston Chronicle* read SALDIVAR GUILTY OF SLAYING SELENA; The *Corpus Christi Caller Times* displayed in huge letters TEARS AND JOY and showed a photo of a Selena fan holding a poster of the singer in one hand and offering a thumbs-up gesture with the other. Throughout much of the nation and in Latin America, the verdict was front-page news.

Primer Impacto had been the only program on television to broadcast the jury's decision live. An unexpected satellite problem interrupted the other networks' transmissions, and their broadcasts were delayed for some time. The *Dallas Morning News* published a huge headline: UNIVISION BROAD- CASTS VERDICT BEFORE RIVAL CHAIN. A copy of the article was faxed to all Univisión affiliates. In Miami, where the net- work's headquarters are based, the executive directors of the network jumped for joy during their weekly meeting because we had beaten the competition.

Now that the verdict had been read, the trial would enter its final phase: The jury would decide Yolanda's pun- ishment. In order to do this, the defense as well as the pros- ecution had to return to court and briefly present opening arguments, witnesses and closing arguments. Only then would the panel of jurors retire to deliberate on the sentence.

Texas law allows much latitude in the sentencing of a person convicted of first-degree murder who does not have a previous criminal record. The possibilities ranged from conditional probation to life imprisonment. The death penalty was not an option since Yolanda had not been charged with a double felony. Even so, many wanted her sent to death row or at the least put away for eternity. When I arrived at the court building the following Tuesday, a crowd was already gathered in front. They carried signs written in English and Spanish, asking for the maximum penalty in the crudest of ways. KILL THE PIG, said one. Another said: 100 YEARS FOR YOLANDA.

On Tuesday, October 24, both sides presented their opening arguments. Valdez wanted to convince the jury that the convicted murderer did not deserve to rejoin society ever again because she had the potential to commit other crimes. He intended to bolster his argument by presenting witnesses who would show that Yolanda had stolen from Selena after a long period of committing fraud. But the judge wanted to hear the witnesses' testimonies without the jury present in order to determine if the prosecution's evidence was admissible in court. Westergren then gave the jury the afternoon off and the testimonies that followed were heard with the jury in absentia.

Valdez presented the Corpus Christi police officer in charge of the fraud section who had carried out an investigation on some suspicious checks from the Selena Etc. boutiques. After reviewing the checks signed by Yolanda and studying the various transactions, he concluded that based on his experience, he believed she had committed fraud. But the expert's professional opinion was only that—there still was no tangible proof of the crime.

This was followed by the testimony of the accountant of Selena Etc. She discovered that Yolanda had signed checks, payable to cash, to pay invoices from a number of suppliers. The checks had been cashed, but the funds had never reached those to whom they were owed. The insinuation was that Yolanda had kept the cash. During his cross-examination, Tinker got the witness to admit that she had started her job with the company after Selena's death, and therefore it was impossible for her to know how the singer managed her business. In other words, it was possible that Yolanda had carried out certain cash transactions—not to steal, but because she was following Selena's instructions. Perhaps the singer needed the cash to cover personal expenses and managed her finances that way for her own convenience. Without Selena, it was impossible to prove otherwise.

The prosecutor also called on Dr. Faustino Gómez, the San Antonio dermatologist for whom Yolanda had worked between 1980 and 1983. The doctor said he had fired Yolanda after discovering that $9,200 was missing from his accounts. Gómez sued his former employee, but she was never convicted of theft since an agreement was reached outside of court.

By this time Westergren was losing his patience. In an impatient tone, he questioned the prosecutor's strategy of presenting weak evidence. As an employee, Yolanda's motives in these situations had been unclear, but she had not necessarily committed any crimes. Referring to the boutique business, the judge concluded: "There is no evidence that Yolanda Saldívar ended up with any of this money … It would be different if she had forged the checks, but she had the authority to write the checks." He was clearly irritated. Even so, Westergren allowed the allegations to be presented to the jury.

That night, Valdez and his team apparently rethought their moves in the courtroom, realizing that the embezzlement accusations would be difficult to prove at this point. Rather than present weak evidence and risk losing a potential appeal in the murder case, they scrapped their plans and all but abandoned the embezzlement angle. As Jorge Rangel said on our show, the jury already had plenty of reasons to severely punish the criminal.

And so on the following day, Valdez only called on Dr. Faustino Gómez. He had barely managed to say that

Yolanda was not a law-abiding citizen when Tinker, during cross, got him to admit that he had not had any contact with Yolanda in more than a decade. The judge had limited the testimony relating to Yolanda's character to incidents that had taken place within the last ten years.

It was now the defense's turn, and it was their last chance to prevent the law from coming down with its full force on Yolanda Saldívar. Tinker went out of his way to show that the life his client had led before March 31 had been exemplary.

First he called on Fernando Saldívar, Yolanda's brother, to testify. Then he called on Fernando's best friend. Both men are veterans of the Vietnam War. Since the jury foreman was a former marine, it is obvious that the choice of witnesses was careful. Both emphasized that Yolanda was a good person—religious, honest and hardworking—who had inspired her nephews to pursue an education and helped her community by raising money for the local Little League.

But Tinker saved the most moving testimony for last. Frank Saldívar, Yolanda's father, had not entered the courtroom until that day because of his delicate state of health. Ironically, that very day, October 25, 1995, was his sixty-ninth birthday. Just as his family had feared, far from being a joyous one, the day was one of the worst in his life. I had returned to the Univisión trailer to prepare for the show and heard his words through the speakers allowing us to listen to the events in the courtroom.

Yolanda's father called her "our baby, the light of my eyes and my heart." With his voice breaking, he told the jury in perfect English how good she had been to the family. Then without knowing he was violating the rules of the court, he addressed the jurors directly and asked them to raise their hands if they believed in God. Valdez objected. But perhaps because of the emotional gravity of the moment, he didn't press the issue. Frank Saldívar excused himself and only managed to say to the panel, "If you have sons and daughters and believe in God, you know we are all brothers. Two lives have been lost here."

A heavy silence descended on us. I could see that our producers were nearly in tears. I was barely able to contain myself from crying, too.

In his closing statement, Tinker emphasized that a sentence should not be based on an eye for an eye. He quoted the Bible and how it favors forgiveness instead of vengeance and recalled how on the tapes Yolanda, clearly torn by Selena's death, could be heard asking for forgiveness. As far as Tinker was concerned, society had already punished her. He finished by saying that Yolanda did not represent a menace to the rest of the world and asked the jury to be kind and to consider probation as a possible sentence.

It was Mark Skurka's task to make the prosecution's final statements. He emphasized that the last thing Selena heard in the final moments of her life was Yolanda screaming "Bitch!" at her as she chased her. The prosecutor recognized that both families had suffered, but made the differences clear. The Quintanillas would never see their daughter again; the Saldívars at least could visit theirs in prison. And he wrapped his statements up with a firm voice, saying there could be no clemency, that Yolanda should be given as punishment that which she had taken away—"*Life* ... that's why she deserves *life* ... in prison."

The jury left the courtroom to deliberate.

Then everything took on a surreal quality. The tension-filled atmosphere that had been present from the first day seemed to dissipate instantly. Suddenly the mood seemed lighter. Everyone was behaving in a friendly and relaxed manner. Jorge Rangel said that it looked like a party. Valdez, Tinker and even Yolanda started signing autographs for the journalists, court employees and spectators in the courtroom. While she waited for the verdict, Yolanda lunched at the defense table, and the Quintanillas retreated to the courthouse balcony to greet the people on the street. The only serious ones were the Saldívars, who kept their distance, praying.

The jury members asked Westergren to let them go home to reflect overnight since they could not reach an agreement. The judge denied the request and sequestered the twelve jurors. Without disclosing its name, he sent them to a hotel to spend the night. That same evening, a press party was held and it so happened that it took place in the same hotel where the jurors were staying. We found this out much later. So close and yet so far!

That evening, *Primer Impacto* aired our exclusive interview with Dr. Ricardo Martínez, who we'd finally managed to secure. I would have liked to have interviewed him personally, but since the sentence could be announced at any moment, I could not leave for Monterrey. Instead we sent our reporter Ricardo Vela.

Perhaps because they shared the same first name, the two Ricardos got along well. Though they chatted for only a few hours, the doctor told Vela many interesting things.

He told him how he had met the singer, describing Selena's financial dealings in Monterrey and how "her father never agreed that she should open a business in Mexico. He managed all her money and if he did not agree, he would not give her money for what she needed to do." He recognized that Abraham would become enraged at his declarations, but it did not seem to matter to him.

Regarding Selena and Yolanda, Martínez said, "The relationship between Selena and Yolanda was that of boss and employee, but for sure, there was a great amount of trust in it. However, near the end I noticed that Selena did not have as much trust; the relationship had cooled. Selena had problems with her family because of that friendship."

"And what can you tell us about the events prior to March 31?" asked Vela.

"Yolanda called me on March 29. She spoke with my secretary and mentioned that she had been raped and that she had lost some important papers belonging to Selena. I didn't believe her. Then Selena called me on March 30, told me about the alleged rape and said that Yolanda had asked her to come see her at the motel alone, and I advised her to bring someone with her." After a moment's thought he added, "I never would have trusted in Yolanda Saldívar."

He said that on the morning of Selena's death, the singer had called him again. He had not been able to come to the phone because he was in surgery. They were never to speak again.

"The friendship between Selena and Yolanda," he said, "was the result of the loneliness that surrounded Selena. That's why Yolanda became her confidante. Because Selena had no friends, since her work did not allow for that, and she needed someone with whom she could let herself be open." He told us that Selena had confessed to him that she wanted to divorce her husband because he gave her no support because they had chosen different paths.

At my request, Vela asked him if Selena and he had been lovers. The doctor became visibly nervous and denied it. When another journalist interviewed him much later, he reacted in the same way, but he was more explicit in this denial.

Due to that exclusive, other media swooped down after Martínez like hawks. He said nothing for a long period, and when he finally decided to reveal more in an interview published in *US* magazine months later, he made some impressive declarations about his relationship with the singer and the role Yolanda had played in everything. I won't disclose all the details now because in order to better understand the situation, it is necessary to know what Yolanda revealed to me in the exclusive interview she would grant me in a matter of weeks.

Martínez was not the only one to speak on our show that night. To everyone's amazement, Selena's mother, who had not said a word since losing her daughter, also broke her long silence. Though she appeared to be frail, she spoke firmly, "I don't hate Yolanda Saldívar. I hate what she did." About the trial she limited herself to saying that no verdict or punishment would ever bring her daughter back.

Marcella Quintanilla was a true lady, worthy of admiration from beginning to end.

On the morning of October 26, Arnold stopped by our trailer. He was convinced that the longer the jury took in agreeing upon a sentence, the lighter the punishment would be and the better it would be for Yolanda. In a few hours he would be proven wrong.

Shortly after that I stood in front of *Primer Impacto*'s cameras on the street awaiting the verdict. I wanted to prevent the news from catching me by surprise and be prepared to go live, if that was necessary, at any given moment. Our technical director had the good sense to connect the IFB I wore to the same system that fed the speakers to all the press, just as we'd done when waiting for the verdict. That is how I found out instantly that the jury had come to an agreement and that the sentence would be announced in a matter of minutes. It was 2:30 in the afternoon.

Inside the courtroom, Rangel also was ready. He would observe everything in detail and later relay it live on our show.

The scene was almost the same as it had been on the day that Yolanda had been found guilty. The courtroom was full, and outside the crowd was calling for the maximum penalty.

The jurors entered the courtroom after having deliberated for nine hours over the course of two days. Westergren asked Yolanda if she wanted to say anything else before the reading of the sentence. She declined.

After a few seconds, the judge's voice was heard: "Life in prison."

Those words brought Yolanda's life, in essence, to an end. She would have to serve a minimum of thirty years in jail before she would be eligible for parole. Her attorney threw his arms around her and she held on to him as she repeated in English, "Oh, Mr. Tinker! Oh, Mr. Tinker!" The Saldívars gave free rein to their sorrow and burst into tears. The Quintanillas did not appear to be happy or relieved. Surely after so many months of agony they were emotionally drained, but they approached the jurors and thanked them for their decision. Then they hurriedly left the courthouse.

Westergren allowed Yolanda's parents to go to their daughter. Juanita hugged her as she told her she loved her. Frank only counseled her to read her Bible and not to forget that one day God would judge her fairly. Yolanda seemed to regress into herself and cried like a little child. Shortly after, the officers led her away in handcuffs. The courtroom was cleared—empty and silent as though nothing had taken place there during the last three weeks.

On the street the scene was quite the opposite. People started to yell rowdily. It seemed as though they were all possessed by the same force. The party went on for hours. I am convinced that this euphoria rubbed many people the wrong way. Marielena Avalos, a thirty-three-year-old receptionist who had been inside the courtroom when the sentence had been announced, commented to a local reporter, "I am Selena's fan, and perhaps if I had been out here with the crowd I would be celebrating. But the public is not aware of what the Saldívar family is going through."

Yolanda's sentence would not bring Selena back to the world, and this final verdict only confirmed that in this tragedy not one but two families had lost their beloved daughters. Yolanda, by killing Selena, had ended her own life.

That afternoon, I felt it was a matter of principle to make that statement on the show. I did it knowing no journalist, throughout the trial, had dared to go up against the popular opinion, one that was marked by an unquenchable thirst for revenge. Rangel and Castillo agreed with me. In their on-air commentaries they said that instead of a day for celebration, it should be a day of reflection. I shared with viewers the saying, "Revenge is the common man's justice; justice is the revenge of the civilized man." The words are not mine, nor have I been able to trace their origin, but they seemed appropriate.

As she left the building, one of the court employees told me in a whisper that she thought the punishment imposed on Yolanda was excessive, especially since it was a first offense. She added that if the victim had been someone else and not a famous individual, the convicted criminal would have received a lighter sentence.

During the final press conference that afternoon, Valdez stated that the people of Corpus Christi had gone to Houston in search of justice and had found it. He promised he would continue investigating the alleged theft by Yolanda from Selena's business and that he would have her tried again in the future for fraud. Shortly after, I saw him in the crowd signing autographs on dollar bills and holding babies like a politician. He was, after all, up for reelection.

The public treated him like a hero. Valdez and his team left the courthouse and went to celebrate at a local Indian restaurant.

Tinker, on the other hand, wore a pained expression on his face. In his brief statements to the press, he announced he would appeal the case. The defense attorney jumped into his car and I suspect he headed for his sailboat. Sailing is his favorite pastime and it is his habit to take to the water when he needs to think and clear his mind.

I called María Elida to see if the family wanted to make an official statement, but I couldn't find her. She and her family had left immediately for their house in San Antonio. I phoned them there and another of Yolanda's sister spoke to me. Crying, Virginia informed me that María Elida, who was diabetic, had experienced a dangerous rise in her blood sugar due to the stressful events and had been hospitalized.

I also tried to locate the Quintanillas, but could not find them either.

Arnold García looked like a lost soul. His eyes were watery; whether it was because he was sad or because he'd had a drink to drown his feelings of disappointment, he was quieter than usual, smoking like a chimney and coughing like never before.

Tina Valenzuela, Tinker's assistant, had also been deeply affected. After all, she and Yolanda had become close in the last few months. I managed to interview her as she was leaving, quickly weaving my way through the tangle of cables in the press area outside the courthouse. As she cried she told me she would always continue to be Yolanda's friend. "I'm not going to forget about her and I'm going to send her pictures of my daughter so she can see her growing up," she assured me.

As soon as the sentence had been announced, one of my confidential contacts sent me the list of jurors with their addresses and phone numbers. We needed to interview one immediately to offer complete coverage. In addition, Alina Falcón had told me that if we didn't find a juror to talk to that same afternoon, I would have to stay another day until I found one. After all this time in Houston, I was exhausted and I wanted to go back home. So I told Alina: "Don't worry. I'll find a juror one way or another, today."

With the list in my hand, I started to phone them one by one. Some had not yet gotten back to their homes, others did not speak a single word of Spanish. And time was against me. Finally I came up with José Estimbo, a Hispanic juror whose command of the Spanish language was not perfect, but certainly comprehensible. I had to convince him to talk to me in front of the camera. At first he refused since he feared he would not keep his part of the promise he shared with the other jurors: that nothing that had been said within the four walls of the room where their deliberations had taken place would ever get out.

"Speak to me about whatever you are allowed to," I told him.

"But won't that bring me problems later?" Estimbo asked me fearfully.

"Why should it," I countered, "if it's all over?"

Finally he agreed. He told me how to get to his house. It was far from the courthouse. I set off quickly, trying to take advantage of the time I had before the live edition of the show for the West Coast, which we still had to broadcast. I had two hours to travel a half hour by car, have the camera equipment set up, interview Estimbo, drive back, edit the segment and air the piece on the show. You have got to be a bit crazy to be in this business!

On the way there, my cameramen turned the radio on. A radio host made reference to the comments I had just made on my show opposing the celebrations on the street. He, too, agreed that we needed to be prudent and perhaps pray for Selena. From that point on the listeners called in and flooded the station's switchboard in support of my comments.

José Estimbo received us at home. He was relaxing with a beer in hand. My cameramen, Angel and Carlitos, worked at the speed of light. My questions had to be quick and to the point. I wanted this interview to take us back to the jurors' deliberations so that we would not have to guess as to what had taken place.

"José, when you started out as a juror, did you think that Yolanda Saldívar was guilty or innocent?"

"Innocent," he answered.

However, after examining the evidence, he said he changed his mind.

"Did you at any point doubt that Yolanda Saldívar had set the gun off by accident?"

"No," he answered, "I think she did it on purpose."

Estimbo explained that for him and other jurors the fact that Yolanda had not put down the weapon and did nothing to aid the victim were the behavior of an assassin, not a friend. For them, Trinidad Espinoza, the Days Inn jan-itor who'd witnessed an emotionless Yolanda pointing the gun at Selena before returning to room 158, was the most convincing witness.

Apparently the jury had reached consensus on Yolanda's culpability early on. Only one member of the jury had difficulty in finding Saldívar guilty of first-degree mur-der and then sentencing her to life in prison. That member of the jury had been an Anglo whose name was Edward Kuhn. Estimbo explained, with obvious pride, how another Mexican American member of the jury managed to con-vince Kuhn on both occasions to change his mind. Throughout the interview, he spoke with such confidence that the only question I had left to ask him was whether his conscience was clear.

"I'll sleep well," he replied.

We left his house running to the car and raced to the courthouse as quickly as possible. We only had a few minutes to edit the interview and go on air. Angel and Carlitos deserve an award for their dedication. They edited the piece in half the usual time. Thanks to them, everything was ready thirty seconds before we went on the air. When I announced that we had statements from one of the Hispanic jurors, I sensed how our competition, just a short distance from us, was left out in the cold. We had beaten them once again. Without a doubt, the exclusive interview with José Estimbo had guar-anteed Univisión the gold medal for being the one news source that had best covered the trial from beginning to end.

The next day when I left for Miami, I thought of Yolanda. I was returning to my own life with a future ahead of me, and at the very same time she was back in jail facing life in prison. She had been convicted without testifying and it did not occur to me that morning on the plane that I would see her again so soon. Much less did it occur to me that she would take the witness stand with me, that I would make her answer the questions the prosecution had not been able to and that through my interview, the world would hear from the mouth of the convicted murderer for the first time what had happened in room 158.

8

The Interview with
Yolanda Saldivar

NOVEMBER 1995

The women who entered the ladies' room at the
Houston airport on November 2 surely must have thought
I was insane. I must have been quite a sight, washing my
hair at the sink in a public restroom. But I didn't care. I had
to focus on my interview with Yolanda, which was finally
going to take place in a few hours. I felt it was my responsibility as a journalist that it be the most important trial-
related interview for a long time to come.

As I looked at myself in the mirror, my hair covered in
shampoo, I reviewed all the recent events that had brought
me to this moment. Yolanda had called me in Miami immediately after the trial, about a week before, to tell me that

she was ready to tell the world her version of the events and fulfill her promise of telling it to only one member of the press. That person was going to be me. We talked on the phone over a period of several days, coordinating the details that would make the interview possible. Our meeting would take place in the Nueces County jail in Corpus Christi. She was being held there until her transfer to the place where she would carry out her sentence: the state penitentiary in Gatesville, Texas.

There were a few hurdles to clear before we reached a final agreement on the conditions of the interview. One of these was that Yolanda wanted to know in advance what questions I would ask her during the interview. All I would tell her was that my questions would probe deeply and would revolve around her relationship with Selena, the events that took place prior to and on March 31 and, of course, the trial. Eventually, she realized that I was not about to give her further details. She was also determined to wear civilian clothes instead of prison garb during the show and would not appear in front of the cameras otherwise. We had to wait for Judge Westergren to issue special authorization for Yolanda to dress in street clothes for the event. Of course, the necessary document took forever to reach us. We were ready to get on the plane to Corpus Christi and one single but necessary piece of paper was nowhere to be found. When I received word that everything was in order, I could hardly believe it. I finally had the exclusive in my hands! That night I could not sleep. In front of millions of viewers, I was about to attempt to decipher the enigma known as Yolanda Saldívar and solve the mystery of what had taken place in room 158.

The morning the interview was to take place, every-thing that could go wrong did. At the last minute, the Miami-to-Houston flight was canceled, and after waiting three hours, we took another one that arrived too late to make the connection to Corpus Christi. Could it be possible that after all this, everything would fall apart because of the airlines? When we landed in Houston, we were informed that we would have to wait for a flight to Corpus that would arrive there much later than we had planned. I looked at the clock and realized that once we arrived in Corpus Christi, I would not have the time to get ready in my hotel room as I had originally planned. The only way I would get to the interview site on time and still look presentable was by using the airport bathroom—and so I found myself looking like a madwoman washing her hair in a public sink.

It was difficult to rinse my hair. In my haste, water ran down onto the floor and I didn't have the time to offer my excuses to the cleaning staff for the mess I had made. Drying my hair was even worse—I had to use paper towels. In all honesty, I don't recommend it. As I carried out the tricky feat, I recalled Yolanda's tone during our most recent phone conversation. She explained that her attorneys did not want her to be interviewed because they planned to appeal the case and did not want to take the risk that she might say something that would interfere with the process. But Yolanda was determined and told me, "Up to now, everyone else has been in charge of the situation. But from now on, I'm going to be the one to control everything." I'd asked myself how that decision would affect the interview and I told myself that she wasn't going to control *me*.

In that conversation, she again spoke specifically about the secret. But she was no longer the vulnerable soul she had been the first time she had mentioned it, when she'd called me after the verdict. Now she was quite calculating. This time, she knew our roles were different; she was talking to a reporter, not just a sympathetic voice on the other end of the phone. She made it clear that her words relating to the secret on that earlier occasion had been off the record—they were to be kept strictly confidential and not used in any kind of coverage. She knew quite well that this would keep me from using the information in a professional capacity.

Yolanda's request that her words be off the record effectively put me in the same situation as a priest—whatever he hears during confession is never to be repeated. In similar fashion, the ethics of good journalism impose sanctions on reporting what has been revealed in confidence. In fact, many of my colleagues have chosen to go to jail rather than to obey a judge's order to reveal the name of a source, or, as was the case here, to reveal what the source said. If a journalist were to divulge this information, she would lose her credibility and would never be trusted again.

All this served to make my interview with Yolanda an even greater personal challenge. I had to clear my mind of all the information I already had about Yolanda, including the information from her I could not use. I wanted to come to this fresh, to put myself in the place of the viewer and approach the subject as if I knew only the bare facts— though of course that was not the case.

As I combed my hair, I began to prepare myself psychologically for my encounter with her. I tried to focus on the approach I would use during the interview. I wanted it to be a conversation, not a confrontation. And I prayed that I'd be able to walk the line between respect and assertiveness without losing my balance. My goal was that the interview would become a dialogue that would make Yolanda say more than everyone expected, more than what she herself had planned to reveal.

When I finished my hair, the flight to Corpus was boarding. On the plane I sat next to my producer, María López, to review the format for the show. When we arrived we went directly to the jail. To our surprise several reporters from the local stations awaited us. They were covering the news that Yolanda was about to break her silence. I have no idea how they found out about the interview, but they were clearly envious that Yolanda was granting us an exclusive. While María López gave instructions to *Primer Impacto*'s technical crew, several reporters asked me for information on what was about to take place. In all honesty, what could I say about an event that had yet to unfold? And I did not want to make any comment that might jeopardize the interview, especially since it would not be aired for several days.

Fortunately we were interrupted by the prison director, who very kindly came out to greet me and then escorted me into the jail. Once inside, he confessed that the journalists we had run into had spent the entire morning complaining because they were not being allowed to speak to Yolanda. What they did not know was that he could do nothing without Yolanda's consent. And she only wanted to talk to me. Yolanda was in control.

The prison director also informed me that a member of Yolanda's defense team was waiting to speak with me before the interview took place. My heart raced and I assumed the worst of possibilities. Yolanda had canceled our interview before the preliminary hearings in Corpus Christi months before at the last minute. Was she about to inform me through one of her lawyers that she had changed her mind yet again?

But I relaxed when I entered Yolanda's jail cell. Arnold García greeted me with his usual smile. "I just wanted to say hello before you started taping," he said.

Yolanda stood behind Arnold wearing her red jacket. "The same one you wore the first day of the trial," I reminded her, just to break the ice. She responded with a smile and admitted that she was surprised at my ability to remember details. She was as nervous as I was.

Tina Valenzuela also was present. She was lending her support to her friend Yolanda on this very important day. I greeted her and we started to make small talk, which helped relieve the initial tension. Yolanda introduced me to the officer in charge of the watch on her cell—she was an avid fan of *Primer Impacto*.

A short while later, a group of security guards came for us. They escorted us to the room where the interview was to take place. Arnold and Tina, as well as the guards, remained outside.

The moment the door shut, Yolanda became visibly nervous. It was a crucial moment for her. While the crew made their final adjustments to the lights, she told me that she was more than ready to tell her "truth." I took the opportunity to remind her that she would face some powerful questions. She responded by telling me that she had no problem with that. Then the moment arrived and the cameras started to roll.

The first question I asked was an obvious one: "Why have you decided to break your silence?" The answer was simple: "I believe that people want to know my story." That was certain, but why wait until now? Yolanda said that her decision had been reached due to a series of odd events. She spoke of how Selena had appeared to her in her dreams, telling her to break her silence, to tell the whole truth. She also insisted she had received an unsigned letter from an anonymous individual who wrote to her about a mystical experience she'd had in which Selena had communicated with her as well. According to the psychic's letter, Selena wanted Yolanda to know there was nothing to forgive her for.

I think I know what this was all about. Yolanda was letting the world know indirectly that the supposed message that Selena had sent her before, through Walter Mercado, was a mistake. You may recall that Walter had said on the show that he had had a psychic communication with Selena. In it the singer said she forgave Yolanda. At the time, Yolanda became enraged by Walter's comment. It seemed unbelievable to me, considering Yolanda's desperate situation—life in prison—that she would still be concerned about an astrologer's statements.

Yolanda produced this letter and read part of it in which Selena supposedly asked her to reveal the entire truth: "Tell my story, tell your story and remember that I'm thanking you a thousand times for your love toward me as though you were my own mother. I know quite well that the blame lies with the person who led us to that room. I know what this person did to you. I know what they did to me. I know you did not want me to die … you and I share many secrets and I give you my permission to reveal them … you no longer need to keep these truths hidden within you…" Yolanda paused briefly to take a deep breath and kept reading the supposed message from Selena. "I will not rest, Mother, I will not move on to the other side until it is all known."

I asked her what the truths were, and for the first time in public, she said that it was part of a mysterious secret. A secret that was supposed to be critical to the events of March 31, 1995. She assured me that the discussion in room 158 of the Days Inn had been about that secret.

I insisted that she reveal it. After all, she already had Selena's permission to do so. Why not clear up what had happened?

"I feel that I'm up against a wall," she said. "I want to tell everything, but I can't because my case is being appealed and my lawyers have told me that it's not prudent to talk about that. When the moment is right, I will reveal all that my daughter wants me to say." I couldn't help but notice that she referred to Selena as *"mi hija"*—her daughter—and that in the letter Selena called her Mother. I asked her to explain this unusual use of the words. "That's what the relationship between the two of us was like; she is my daughter. She called me mama, madre, mom, but she never called me Yolanda," she responded.

I tried to make the matter clear by telling her, "Yolanda, you know that our viewers are going to think that if Selena were alive, she herself could reveal that truth. But she's dead because you killed her…"

"I'm telling you, María … and God and Selena [also] speak for me, that it was all an accident. I am not a cold-blooded murderer. May God forgive those who have accused me of being one. Things did not happen the way the prosecutor said … my attorneys and I believe that he never proved the intent to kill … we won the case."

"But the jurors believed the prosecutor," I insisted.

"Because the members of the jury had already formed their opinion before the trial started." Then with a tone of resignation, she added, "I don't blame them for that, nor do I hold any grudge against them, because Selena doesn't want me to hold grudges."

Instead of digging deeper into the issue of the trial, I wanted Yolanda to clarify once and for all her relationship with the singer. Without warning I asked her, "Are you a lesbian and were you in love with Selena?"

"No," she answered with unshakable confidence. "That's a lie created by two people—Martín Gómez, the designer, and Abraham Quintanilla. I am not a lesbian."

I wanted her to be more specific and asked her, "Do you like men?"

"I like men. I've had boyfriends. And I've never approved of that lesbian stuff. Selena and I would read the Bible together, and in it they speak of love between man and woman. That's the way it should be."

This was one of those moments in the interview in which I felt that Yolanda was sincere and forceful. On this point, she had me convinced. Not so on others.

I tried to clear up another accusation that had been made against her. "Did you ever steal money from Selena? Yes or no?"

She answered me firmly, "I never took a cent from my daughter."

It was an ideal moment to ask her about her friendship with the queen of Tejano music. "I didn't like Tex-Mex music," she recalled. "Baila Esta Cumbia" was the first song to catch her attention, but she didn't know who the performer was. One day her niece took her to a Selena concert. "When I saw her, I was surprised at how much talent she had and how she made people come alive. She had something special that even if you didn't like her music, once you saw her singing, you'd like it," she insisted.

She said that was the day the idea of founding a fan club was born. "All the other artists have fan clubs. Why doesn't somebody start something like this for Selena? It caught my interest because at the time I was a nurse and I saw it as something [so] different that I would enjoy doing."

Yolanda went into details about how the club had been organized, her friendship with Suzette and how, after six months as head of the fan club, she had finally met Selena in December of 1991. "She was kind, very, very kind. Selena is a person who is easy to love," she told me with her face glowing.

"She *is* a person? She *was* a person," I reminded her.

With this she lost her composure and her voice cracked. "I cannot accept that she is not here. Who cares, María, what sentence I get? It doesn't matter. It doesn't matter if they kill me tomorrow or if they lock me away forever … that doesn't matter. My daughter will always be with me."

At that moment I felt I had to find some kind of perspective. "You keep on calling Selena your daughter, and you've told me that it's because you loved her like a daughter. But you understand that our viewers see a woman who calls Selena her daughter when she's not her daughter; who says that she does not accept that a jury found her guilty, because she believes that she won the case, even though she was convicted; and on top of that, does not accept that Selena is dead, because just a while ago you referred to her as though she were alive. Do you understand that people are going to think that you are a person who is out of touch with reality?"

"I understand, but it doesn't matter," she answered, full of emotion. "I'm a walking zombie, María. As far as this life goes, I'm living, but I've died. The days for me are only that, days. I don't live them. For me there is no happiness, no joy, no harmony."

She confessed to me that she cared little for what people might think of her words. Everything for her was over and done with. This being the case, there was only one question to ask.

"Since you were sentenced to life in prison, have you thought about suicide again?"

"Yes," she answered, "but Selena stops me when I dream about her at night."

Once again I felt the ominous reference to an ongoing mental or spiritual communication with the singer. I decided that rather than have the show appear to be an episode from *The Twilight Zone,* it would be wiser to change the topic.

I asked her to look me in the eye and asked, "Did you mean to kill her or not?"

"No, never," she answered, crying.

I knew that Yolanda was and is a person of great religious fervor. I took the opportunity to add, "Are you willing to swear on the Bible, in front of God, that what you say is true?"

"Yes, because my God knows it was an accident … I'm at peace with God and I'm at peace with Selena."

I asked her, "Are you ashamed of what happened?" And she answered, "In a certain way, yes. Things could have been different if only the people close to her had paid attention to her. María, I'm telling you sincerely that Selena was in a lot of pain."

"Why was she suffering, Yolanda, what was happening to her?"

"That's what I can't tell you at this time."

"When are you going to reveal it? After the appeal?"

"Exactly."

The time had come to ask her about the events inside room 158. At the precise moment when I intended to ask her, the videotape came to an end. While it was being changed, Tina entered the room to say good-bye. Before she left she whispered something in Yolanda's ear. And the moment Tina left Yolanda began to cry hysterically. I asked her what had happened, but all she could do was to press her fist into her chest while she yelled, "Please, don't take her away from me. Don't take her away from me." I started to think that someone had died. Everyone discreetly left her alone with the head security guard who had entered upon hearing the commotion and who stayed with her to calm her down.

A bit later we returned to the room. Between sobs, she told me of her new troubles. A prison guard had been suspended—the one in charge of her security. The young woman had become her friend and confidante. They had penalized her for getting too close to "the recluse" and for forgetting that one of her principal duties was to maintain her emotional distance from the prisoners.

"She's the only one who gave me any support here. My parents visit me, but I'm not allowed to touch them. At least I could give her a hug when I got desperate. She would comfort me," Yolanda said.

I was at a loss for words. It was then that I realized the terribly isolating conditions in which she had to live. In order to protect her from the many death threats she had received, Yolanda was not allowed any contact with the other convicts.

Yolanda cried so hard that her makeup was completely ruined, her face stained black by tears from her mascara. María López and I lent her a few items so she could touch herself up. As she did this, I went over to speak in private with the guard who had consoled her. He explained her behavior to me, "In prison, prisoners get very attached to what little they have, whether it's material or emotional. When part of that, no matter how small it may seem, is taken away, they fall apart and go into crisis mode." Then he took a deep breath and told me, "In all my years in the prison system, I have seen a lot of prisoners who claim to be innocent … but up until now, the only one I've believed is Yolanda."

This intrigued me. What could Yolanda have said to convince him? The question was spinning inside my head when I was told that everything was ready for us to continue the interview.

With my questioning, I led her back to the fateful day of March 31 inside room 158. She was tense.

"It's been said that you asked Selena to come to the motel to see you *by herself*. Why did you do that?" I asked.

She denied it. "I didn't tell her that. On the contrary, I begged her not to come to the motel. I never, ever, told her to come to the motel. She came because she wanted to. If I tell you why she came, I will be revealing the truth that I can't speak about." She did not want to say anything else. What was the queen of Tejano music planning to do? Did it have to do with the suitcase full of clothes that was found later in the motel room?

"Yolanda, did you really want to kill yourself that day?"

"Yes. I couldn't continue with the weight of the secret. I didn't want to be part of that, but my daughter would tell me not to leave her alone. María, I never had a daughter; when I saw my daughter cry I felt a pain in my soul. I tried to leave her side three times, but Selena would tell me that if I abandoned her, she would fall apart."

"I don't understand why you would commit suicide over a secret," I told her.

"Because what she was going to do, what we were going to do, wasn't right. I saw it as something very dangerous for me."

"Yolanda, what could be more dangerous than putting a gun to your head?"

"It's [just] that I had already been threatened physically and they had done other things to me … I didn't want to go on. But she asked me not to leave her alone."

"If you had killed yourself, you would have left her, too," I insisted.

"Yes, but I would have taken the secret with me … Understand?"

It was really taking all my effort to follow her logic.

I asked her to tell me how she had decided to pull out the revolver. First off, she claimed that it was Selena who had taken out the gun first.

"Why would that be if you were the one who wanted to commit suicide?" I asked her in disbelief. Yolanda started to explain herself. They were arguing about the secret when Selena grabbed a duffel bag belonging to Yolanda and emptied its contents onto the bed. (Was she perhaps looking for documents or another item that she wanted?)

One of the items that had been in the bag was the revolver. Yolanda put everything back inside the bag—with the exception of the revolver. She handed the bag to Selena and asked her to leave. According to her, Selena was crying profusely because she feared that Yolanda would take her own life. Yolanda promised her friend that she would never reveal the secret, "Then Selena got on her knees, wrapped her arms around my legs and said, 'Don't leave me. Don't leave me.' I told her, 'I can't take it anymore. If I'm not going to help you, then I'm not helping anybody else.' I repeated, 'Daughter, I want you to leave … Go.' And she didn't want to leave, María. The door was open. Then she told me, 'Mother, let's talk [about it].' But I told her she wasn't going to convince me."

Yolanda kept repeating herself, describing the incident, and she seemed possessed by the same emotion of that terrible moment. I asked her to get to the point. "So what happened then? You say it was an accident. Show me with your hands how it happened, what you did with the gun."

She hesitated for an instant. What followed was not to be believed. Yolanda proceeded to relive every second of the event, with one gesture after another. Her hand movements were those of someone who was picking up a gun and pointing it to her temple to shoot herself. She said in a desperate voice, "Selena went to the door to close it so we could talk…" Suddenly her tone changed dramatically and I heard a cold and calculating Yolanda. "…It was then when I told her, 'Don't close the door.'" Then she finished almost casually, "…Then the gun went off [by itself]." Noticing the three distinct changes in the tone of her voice during her statement, I felt I was witnessing three different personalities. I don't know if the viewers saw that. There are certain subtleties that are lost to the camera, but since I had her right in front of me, I can assure you that is what took place.

It was also with these words that Yolanda contradicted herself. What we had heard her say during the siege in the truck was very different. In the version she gave to the police officers who were trying to negotiate her surrender, she maintained that she had told Selena to *close* the door, not to leave it open.

"What did you do after the gunshot?"

"I was in shock."

"You didn't think you had wounded her?"

"No," she countered. "I only saw that she left [the room]."

"Why did Selena run like someone who's afraid? Why didn't she turn around and say to you, 'Yolanda, what have you done to me? I'm wounded.'"

"Because everything happened so fast," she answered. "If someone had shot me, I, too, would have run for help."

"Why didn't she ask *you* for help? You're trained as a nurse. Who better than you?"

"I don't know. I'm telling you that it all happened so fast. I went out after her, and at that point I couldn't even see her." She was irritated at my insistence.

"Yolanda, why did you leave the room with the gun in your hand?"

"Because I didn't want it to go off again." She denied that she had chased down Selena, pointing the gun at her the way some of the trial witnesses had described.

I reminded her that during the trial, the prosecution had concluded that one of her most incriminating acts was leaving the room with the gun in her hand. According to the prosecutors, when a person fires off a gun accidentally, they tend to let go of the weapon to prevent it from going off again. They don't usually run around with the defective weapon in their hands in order to avoid hurting someone. Her justification to me was this: She took the weapon with her so that others would not be harmed since she, as the owner of the weapon, would be held responsible.

I raised another detail that had managed to convince the jury of her guilt: the fact that she was a nurse and had not called 911 to request medical attention for Selena.

"How do they know I didn't call?" she asked me.

I answered with another question, "You called 911?"

"I can't discuss that."

"If you called 911, why didn't your defense [team] use that?"

"Because I didn't have to prove my innocence. The burden of proof fell on the prosecutor."

"But what better way to settle the matter than saying in court, 'Gentlemen, this woman called for help. Here's the transcript of the phone call'?"

She tried to change the topic but I would not let her.

"If a call was made, there would be a recording of the call. But there isn't one."

"I can't talk about that because of my appeal," she countered.

Tired of her evasive answers, I took another tack. "You say you didn't know Selena was hurt…"

"I didn't know it," she assured me.

"But there was blood on the carpet in the room."

"I was so frightened I didn't see it."

In order to end the game I told her, "So if you didn't think Selena was hurt, it makes sense that you wouldn't have called 911 to ask for help." I wanted to get her to admit what was obvious—that she had never called. Once again, her answer was evasive. "I didn't know she was wounded. That's why I went out to find her, and when I couldn't [find her], I thought, Oh, I'm so glad that the bullet didn't hit her. I got in the truck to keep on looking for my daughter. Yes, I took the gun with me because it was my gun."

We talked about the nine hours she spent in the truck the day of the siege. She insisted that an injustice had been committed against her. "Only five hours were recorded on tape. Where are the other four? From the beginning I was saying it was an accident, but that was never recorded."

I surprised her by asking about Dr. Ricardo Martínez's role. She did not want to offer any details. "I can't reveal it to you. I'd like to, but I can't. He's part of the secret."

I asked her to clear up one of the great mysteries of this whole affair—the ring that fell out of Selena's hand as she lay dying on her way to the hospital.

The first thing Yolanda warned me of was that "many tales have been told about the ring, but none of them is true." The ring was part of the secret she did not want to reveal.

"Wherever we went, Selena would tell me, 'If you see [an imitation] Fabergé egg, buy it for me.' She had a large collection [of decorative eggs and related objects] and all it lacked was a ring."

Yolanda admitted that she had paid for the jewelry with the boutique's credit card, but she insinuated that she was not the real buyer. "When she wanted me to do something, I'd go ahead and do it. She was quite ill in January and she asked me, 'Mother, I don't have any T-shirts. Go and buy me some.' I bought her twenty."

As fate would have it, a short while after the interview other people would name the person who had supposedly ordered the purchase of the ring in order to present it to Selena as a gift. Yolanda had been used as the go-between.

But here we had a new revelation: What had Selena been sick with in January? Being able to foresee the answer, I told her in frustration, "Don't tell me that that's part of the secret, too?"

Bingo! That was the answer she gave me. Later, I learned that all this mystery was nothing more than the simple liposuction Dr. Martínez had performed on the singer. Since he was involved, I suppose that is why she had said it was part of the great secret.

One question regarding the ring had now been answered: It had not been a gift from Chris. "They had problems during the months I spent working with Selena," she said, and added that her friend felt "very alone, too alone" and that she suffered. According to Yolanda, Chris gave her no support to such a degree that supposedly Selena had told her that "there are two people who love me for who I am, not for the money I make or for what I can do in the future. Those two are you and Dr. Martínez."

"Are you telling me that Selena did not mention her own mother, whom she loved so much?"

Unexpectedly, Yolanda asked me for permission to send Selena's mother a message via our cameras. She immediately turned so she could be face-to-face with the lens. With calculated and dramatic control, she paused briefly as she kept her eyes steady, looking into the camera. It seemed that she knew already the dramatic effect her words would have. "Mrs. Quintanilla, in my heart I beg your forgiveness for what I have done, but I tried to tell you what Selena was going through. When I was at the point of revealing every-thing, Selena interrupted us. I asked you to call me, but you never did. Later, your daughter asked me not to tell you or your husband anything about what was happening. All she asked was that I give her my support. I was ready to lose my friendship with Selena in order to make everything known to you, but you did not want to hear me out. I am not blam-ing you, but I did try to speak with you. Forgive me."

Her words brought a whole new dimension into view. Now that she had brought up the Quintanilla family, I fol-lowed her lead.

"Abraham Quintanilla—what does that name mean to you?" I asked her. She answered immediately, almost letting on that she had given much thought to the answer in the loneliness of her jail cell.

"He's a human being, like you and I, [a person] who makes mistakes. Being able to accept them is something else entirely."

I wanted her to cover the topic in depth. "What mistakes has he made in your opinion?" She said, "I can't reveal them, but let me tell you, now I know why his nieces would tell me the man was a savage." The word she used shocked me.

"Savage?" I asked, thinking that I had misunderstood her.

She assured me, "That's what the family called him, but I didn't understand why."

I reminded her that in the tapes during the siege she could be heard accusing Quintanilla of having raped her, something he completely refuted in court under oath. "He did indeed rape me," she came back with great conviction. She did not want to reveal how or when the assault was supposed to have taken place. I explained that without proof or a police report, her accusation was unfounded. But she insisted that it had indeed happened and that Selena wanted her to report her own father to the authorities. "She wanted me to reveal the whole truth." I pointed out that it was quite difficult to convince people that a daughter would want to harm her own father. "People are going to believe what they want, but that is the truth," she concluded.

I mentioned that I had found the piece of paper the officers had passed to one another as they negotiated her surrender—the one with the word "abortion" written on it. Surely she must have mentioned it during the four hours of the siege that were not on tape. She did not want to address the issue. "I can't reveal anything about it, María."

I switched to a less serious topic so we could continue the conversation. "Have you listened to Selena's music again?" She answered that by chance she had heard the song "I Could Fall in Love" on the radio in jail. She said she had been happy to hear it and that the words of the song were somewhat related to the secret.

The entire situation was more than confusing, and Yolanda knew it. Frustratingly, she was adding new questions to the ones we already had, and not answering any of them by using the secret as an excuse. I tried to to get her to be specific. "Tell me, Yolanda, exactly what was going on?" She would come back with another vague answer, "I could see the danger ahead, she didn't … Selena was very noble, very ingenuous…" I reminded her that for the jury, *she* represented the real danger that Selena did not see. Faced with my comment, she stated, "I'm not referring to that type of danger ... but to something that was going to turn things around and cause her to suffer." In every instance, she wanted to give the impression that her role was to protect the singer.

Yolanda had brought a poem she had written to Selena three days after having shot her to death. When she showed it to me, I could not help but notice that it was written in Spanish on the same kind of yellow paper as the letter from the psychic who had supposedly received the message from Selena. I did not say a word. She read it with tears in her eyes:

> On the day of the 31st of March,
> You, my beloved friend, confessed to me
> that the day you were gone I would tell of your sad life.
> But I will tell you, my soul,
> that the bigger pain is your great secret,
> that I recognize is beyond my reach.
> Selena,
> I don't have the courage to tell anyone,
> as much as I would like to, I don't have the courage,
> I walk in the land of the living dead.

"I carry that poem in my soul. It's the only thing that gives me any comfort, any strength to keep going. It gives me hope that one day I will see my daughter in heaven," she continued as she cried. Later, she remembered with great resentment and pain the attacks on her by the public. "Selena would never take pleasure in condemning someone; Selena would never be happy if someone were to be called a monster."

The interview was coming to an end. We spoke about her family. "I suffer a lot for them," she said with deep emotion, "because they don't deserve to be in pain like this. No one deserves to suffer like this. My conscience is clean. My family and friends know that."

I asked her how she felt when people rushed out to the streets to celebrate her conviction and her sentence. "I feel that what's happened to me is what happened to Jesus Christ. He was condemned before he said a single word."

She appeared to be satisfied with the way that Douglas Tinker had carried out her defense. But, I asked her, why didn't her defenders reveal the secret if that was the reason for her conviction? "Because I forbade it," she said, and she did not regret having done so. Nor was she sorry that the defense had played the game of all or nothing, taking away her options by betting her freedom on the jury's not being able to find her guilty of the single charge of first-degree murder. After the verdict, she had been sure that they were going to give her the maximum penalty, she said, "Because people are in pain and I don't blame them. People don't want to accept reality as it is. They're blind and poisoned by the ideas that have been put in their minds ... Ironically, those responsible for Selena's death washed their hands, are free and people are giving them their support." Even now, as she sat in jail, Yolanda seemed to be denying she'd played any part in the singer's death.

She gave me the impression that she believed that public opinion about her would change once she revealed the secret, but she ultimately denied it. "I'm not here to change that kind of thinking in anyone's head. The day I'm ready to reveal all, I'll do it with facts, with papers, with proof in hand, to show the people what really happened, what Selena was planning. I know that my God, Selena, my family and my true friends know I'm not a monster. I'm a human being."

I didn't like the fact that she claimed Selena was planning something. It could be easily misinterpreted. I asked her to be more specific, but she wasn't. "Selena was only human and that's why I ask the public not to judge her when the truth is revealed … because she was human like the rest of us."

The interview was over. After three hours (the interview would be edited down to one hour), we were all emotionally exhausted. As we removed our microphones, Yolanda whispered in my ear, "Remember what I told you about suicide?" I nodded in agreement. She went on to tell me that "…well, not only have I considered doing it again. I think about it every day." I was struck numb.

At that moment, guards came to lead her away to her cell. I asked them to let me continue my private conversation with her for a few more moments. When they left us alone, I told her that if the thought of killing herself came up again, to think of the great harm she would cause her parents. Yolanda changed the topic abruptly and asked me if the interview would help my show's ratings. I told her that *Primer Impacto* had always had high ratings, but that, without a doubt, the interview she had granted would be one of the high points for its viewers. With a smile, she came back with, "Oh, it's just that I wanted it to help you."

That comment couldn't help but catch my attention. I looked her in the eyes and she seemed sincere. It puzzled me that this woman, who had so many problems, would worry about me. I honestly felt sorry for her. Here I was, triumphantly walking out with my videotapes in hand, and she was being marched off to face the walls of her cell for the rest of her days. We expressed our good-byes Latin style, with a kiss on the cheek.

I sat down to think about the interview while my colleagues packed up. We had our photos taken with the guards, who were big *Primer Impacto* fans.

Shortly afterward, I saw an officer walk by holding Yolanda's red jacket, folded to perfection. I knew right away what it meant and tried to imagine Yolanda dressed in her prison uniform.

Ready to Broadcast the Interview

Something very curious happens when two or more persons who work in the TV industry find themselves seated at the same table: The only topic of conversation is television. And that night just hours after our interview had ended, there was so much to talk about that it was hard to know where to begin.

Fortunately, my producer and I dined with Jorge Rangel and his charming wife, Lupe. He was more than eager to find out what Yolanda had told us. Just like us, he had by that point become addicted to the case. We gave him an advance preview over dinner and enjoyed every one of his reactions. After each revelation, he would open his eyes wide and say, "No! She told you that!"

Lupe was marvelous. Apart from keeping us from getting carried away, she added her usual intelligent comments. Because she was an outsider and totally objective, her words were especially encouraging.

Of course, that night we held on to the videotapes of the interview as though they were pieces of gold. We did not want to lose them or have them stolen. María López and I even took them with us when we went to the rest room, a habit of the trade.

The next day we returned to Miami early. From the moment we entered the Univisión offices, we began work on promoting the interview, which we planned to air in a few days' time.

Univisión's executives responded with understandable paranoia, which seems to appear out of nowhere when you know you've landed a big scoop. "Are you sure Yolanda isn't talking to anyone else?" They were afraid that someone would steal our lead and that we would promote the story as our exclusive only to find that another network had beaten us to the punch while we edited the piece. I reassured them on every possible count, but I crossed my fingers anyway. Later other networks started calling us— including a German one—asking for several clips from the interview "in order to promote the exclusive from your show." That's an old trick if ever there was one.

The phones on my desk would not stop ringing. One of the first calls was from Yolanda. I won't deny that my reaction to her was one of surprise and concern. Very anguished, she asked me to cut the sequence where I had asked her if Abraham Quintanilla had raped her. Her lawyers were furious because if her answer was to be broadcast on the air, her appeal would be in danger. So I edited it out (even though her comments were very similar to what she had said on the negotiation tapes) because she had never set any limits as to what I could or could not ask, and she had never asked for anything in exchange for the interview.

Newspapers and magazines from all around the country were asking me for interviews. They wanted to know what Yolanda had revealed. I would tell them just enough to pique their interest. Then with a touch of humor, I recommended that they watch *Primer Impacto* in a couple of days. On the street, people who had seen some of the promotional spots we were running stopped me to ask the same quesion. A security guard told me he was planning to take his portable TV to work so he could watch the interview while on duty—a good omen, without a doubt. Later I found out that many people had canceled dinners and dates to stay home in front of their TVs.

Finally, the long-awaited evening arrived. At home I opened a bottle of champagne that Jorge Rangel had given me to celebrate the occasion and I toasted with a group of my most special friends—the ones who never fail to give me their honest opinion, no matter what they think. Fortunately, they loved the interview. And as it turns out, their reactions were shared by the millions of viewers who had tuned in to *Primer Impacto* that evening. The interview was seen by approximately 4.5 million people, receiving a 29-point national

Nielsen rating and becoming one of the five top-rated programs in the history of Spanish-language television. These numbers do not include the millions of viewers who watched in Latin American countries nor the millions who saw it when it was broadcast again two weeks later.

My friends' stamp of approval was validated by the telephone, which rang nonstop during the commercial breaks. One of the first to call was Jorge Rámos, the anchor for Univisión News, a dear colleague and friend and, above all, a veteran of many important interviews. Rámos is considered the Peter Jennings of the Hispanic world. His compliments were quite gracious, and he told me that he had liked how well balanced the program had been. He finally confessed that I had him "glued to the television set and I can't unglue myself." His phone call was immensely reassuring; it's hard to impress a professional like Jorge.

Alina Falcón also called me to say she was more than pleased with the show. She had been behind me from day one and I had delivered for her. The next morning, I sent flowers to my producer, María López, who hadn't stopped working since we'd landed the exclusive.

The show was seen by several jurors whom we had gathered together especially for this event. After watching the interview, they told us with conviction that nothing Yolanda had said changed their opinion that she was guilty.

But the best measure of the show's success came the next morning. The entire country was asking what the famous secret was. It was difficult for me to go out, because everywhere I went—from the bakery to the hairdresser, whether seeing friends, neighbors or people from work—

people asked me what I thought about the secret and other questions that had been left unanswered. They were busily analyzing Yolanda's words for every conceivable meaning. The interview was front-page news in many of the nation's important newspapers. Radio stations opened the airwaves to broadcast callers' opinions. Without my wanting or expecting it to, the interview had become an incredible cultural phenomenon and the secret was the main topic of conversation in cities from coast to coast for several days. We had set off an unexpected chain reaction of arguments, questions and answers.

In the middle of all this, Ray Rodríguez, president of Univisión, phoned me. He had kind words for me, but then he got straight to the point: "What is the secret?" he asked. I smiled, thinking how unbelievable it was to have such an important man intrigued by the secret. Then he congratulated me because "every time Yolanda would say something and I would think of a follow-up question, you would ask that very question as though you were reading my thoughts." (What I wouldn't give to be able to read the mind of the top executive at the world's most powerful Spanish-language network! Maybe I could send him a psychic message to give me a raise.)

That night, María Elida called me with Yolanda also on the line. Yolanda sounded upset. The prison guards had told her that she seemed evasive and that I had been too aggressive. As I was about to answer her, her alloted amount of time on the prison phone ran out.

I gave interviews to the media from the United States, Mexico and Latin America. One is worth mentioning because it has a funny twist. On *Sábado Gigante,* the enormously successful Spanish-language variety show hosted by Don Francisco (Mario Kreutzberger), Don Francisco himself tried every trick in the book, and then some, to get me to talk about the famous secret. By sheer coincidence, that particular segment of the show had been sponsored by Secret, the deodorant.

I was very proud that we had topped off our coverage by offering viewers something so substantial and important. We had succeeded, and now it was time to rest for a bit. I went to New York to spend Thanksgiving with my mother and other members of my family. It was a wonderful respite and I had much to be thankful for.

But I never imagined the surprise that was waiting for me back in Miami.

10

Abraham Quintanilla Responds

DECEMBER 1995

When I returned from my Thanksgiving vacation, I found an unexpected message on my desk: Abraham Quintanilla had called me personally and needed to talk to me right away. I returned his call immediately. I truly expected to hear an angry man who would complain to me bitterly about the interview with Yolanda. But I heard the opposite—a warm greeting and a calm voice. The first words out of his mouth: "At the beginning I was opposed to your giving this woman a forum so she could tell her story on television, but after seeing the program, I changed my opinion." Although he did not say so specifically, I assumed that meant he had found the show objective and balanced.

After the formalities, he got to the point and in a quiet, almost resigned voice asked, "Why are you people so determined to dig up things that don't exist?" The question could not have been more unfair, but because of the tone he used I did not feel insulted. I answered him calmly: "Mr. Quintanilla, I honestly don't know what you're referring to." What he told me next sounded odd and unbelievable. He said there was a man in Monterrey who was trying to extort money from him in exchange for his silence. If he didn't get the money, he would reveal to *Primer Impacto* everything he knew about Selena's supposed secret. This threatening stranger assured Quintanilla that he was already in negotiations with my show to conduct an interview.

I interrupted him. Politely, but firmly, I assured him that at the moment we were not investigating anything or anyone in Monterrey. "OK. I believe you," he answered me. It couldn't help but come to my attention how easy it had been to convince him. I had the feeling that Abraham was fishing for information and that he knew very well that *Primer Impacto* was not involved with this stranger. Curiously, shortly after our conversation, the alleged blackmailer would go public and I would be the one to speak to him, though it would be over the phone and not on camera.

As it turned out, the real motive for Abraham Quintanilla's call had been something else. He was indignant because what Yolanda had said about the existence of a secret could be easily misinterpreted. In his opinion her intentions had been malicious, and he explained that he was now suffering the consequences. The weekend of my interview, someone had approached him in a restaurant and asked if the relationship between him and Selena had been an incestuous one. Abraham had almost had a heart attack. The one "responsible for that lie" had been Yolanda. "That woman is manipulative. There's no secret. You're an intelligent woman. You know she's lying," he said as though looking for my support.

I explained that it was the public, not I, who should decide if Yolanda was lying, reminding him that people are not stupid and are aware if someone is lying or, at the very least, not being consistent in what they say.

Since he sounded so tormented, I tried to comfort him. "Mr. Quintanilla, I don't understand why you are torturing yourself like this since you got what you asked for— Yolanda is behind bars."

"I'm ready to forget all this, but before that, I'm going to speak one last time. I'm ready to talk to you and give you proof of all the things she was doing. How she was stealing. I'll show you copies of the checks and all the rest. Documents no one has ever seen."

"When?" I asked him.

"In a week," he assured me.

Abraham had every right to counter the charges that Yolanda had leveled against him. But given his history of attacking my show, I found it ironic that he would ask me to interview him. I was pleased. It seemed I'd finally convinced him of our desire to provide objective and complete coverage.

The interview involved yet another frenzied trip to Texas, sending equipment and technicians halfway across the country, and once again it seemed as though everything was going to fall apart at the last minute: Abraham had a business emergency to tend to in another town. The interview would not take place in Corpus Christi as we had originally planned, but in San Antonio, at a hotel near the city's Riverwalk.

Abraham was especially gracious and open. He greeted me with a bear hug, very effusive. In fact, when he saw that the cameraman with me was the same one he had thrown out of the press conference in Houston, he approached him and apologized, then had his picture taken with him. He was another person entirely.

As we adjusted the lighting and got ready to begin, we made small talk to relax. I asked him if he was bothered by the negative reputation he had earned for his frequent outbursts. He told me with a smile, "Sometimes I come across as aggressive because in my business you have to be that way. The music scene is full of sharks."

I also asked him why he always wore dark glasses, which seemed to set a barrier between him and the rest of the world. "People say it's so they don't know I'm watching them," he said laughing. "But the truth is that they were prescribed by the doctor because light hurts my eyes."

Abraham asked me not to talk on camera about Yolanda's accusation of rape. I had not planned to do so and there was no reason to mention the topic. He already had denied it in court, and there was neither proof against him nor a formal complaint. "Look, how am I going to rape her with a wife as pretty as mine?" he commented, half joking, half angry.

The moment he mentioned his wife in the conversation, he paused and his voice changed. Abraham told me that his wife was in a fragile emotional state. Marcella Quintanilla rarely got out of bed. She lived in a permanent state of depression. And when she did manage to get out of bed, any reminder of Selena was a major setback. She was trying to pick up the pieces of her life, but the pain of her immense loss was always with her.

When the cameras started to roll, the first thing Abraham did was to explain the reason for the interview: "I feel I have to defend my daughter's image, since she's not here to defend herself. And my family is very hurt that this woman, Yolanda, is appearing on TV all over the world telling lies."

I asked him to tell me which of Yolanda's statements had disturbed him the most. "All the things she said are so very absurd. For example, implying that what was in that letter came from Selena, that Selena speaks to her in her dreams, and calling Selena, 'Daughter' and Selena calling her 'Mother.'"

When I asked him how his wife had reacted, he told me, "Any person in his right mind can see [Yolanda] has a screw loose."

About the secret: "It's pure crap. It's all fabrications from that woman's mind. She killed my daughter and she doesn't want it to end there. She wants to hurt my wife. She wants to hurt Selena's husband. I don't know what that woman's problem is, and I can't understand her thinking."

Abraham had spent months personally investigating Yolanda's supposed crimes against the fan club. Now he was finally going to show me the evidence.

"If you look at this"—he showed me several documents—"the fan club had a secretary, a treasurer, a whole board, in fact. However, Yolanda opened the club's bank account under María Elida's, her sister's, name, when she wasn't even a member of the fan club. We asked her why she had done that."

"And what was her answer?" I asked him.

"Her answer was that the bank hadn't allowed her to open an account under her name."

"Why not?"

"'Well, I don't know,'" Quintanilla answered in a mocking voice, imitating Yolanda, and continued. "There's no logic there. Anybody with a hundred dollars can go to a bank and open a checking account. So then why was Yolanda doing this? If you take a look at this"—he told me, showing me some checks—"it was supposedly María Elida Saldívar who was writing out the checks, but there was nothing on the detail line to show what the checks were for."

"Which one ought to write down if you want to keep your accounts in order," I added.

"Right!" he answered, excited that I could see where he was heading. "If we look here at Yolanda's signature and you compare it with María Elida Saldívar's…"

"They look very much alike, if not identical," I said, completing his thought.

"It's the *same* signature," he finished up—with a tone of voice that left no room for doubt.

His conclusion was that it had been Yolanda who had written the checks using her sister's name. She would then cash them and keep the money. According to him, there was more to be suspicious about. "She made the fan club files vanish. When we went looking for them they did not exist. She herself once said on TV that the club supposedly had eight thousand members, and each had paid twenty-two dollars … Where is the money? Where are the files?"

Abraham continued presenting his proof. He showed us a letter which appeared to be in Yolanda's handwriting, signed with María Elida's name. In the letter, María Elida informed the bank that she had to close the club's account because of a major problem: One of the club members, an Ivonne Perales, had been sent to deposit three thousand dollars in the bank, but she had not done so and was nowhere to be found. María Elida supposedly had discovered too late that Ivonne and the money were missing. Thinking that the money was still in the account, she had written checks for Yolanda against the account. The checks had been cashed by Yolanda even though there were no funds in the account. For that unfortunate reason, the letter stated, she was closing the account and informing the bank that they would have to cover the checks.

"When Selena, Suzette and I confronted her in March and asked her who Ivonne Perales was, do you know what her answer was? *'I don't know, Mr. Quintanilla,'*" he said, once again mocking Yolanda's voice. "But how could she not know? She didn't trust the club treasurer to handle the money, but she trusted a total unknown to deposit three thousand dollars. I told her, 'You can tell that lie to someone else.'"

Excited, he finished by saying that Ivonne Perales did not exist because none of the others in charge of the club's management had met her. According to him, that is how Yolanda stole six thousand dollars: three thousand dollars belonging to the fan club and were never deposited and three thousand dollars in checks that were paid out by the bank, despite the fact that the account was overdrawn.

Abraham was convinced that Yolanda began to plan her crime after their meeting on March 9, 1995, when he threatened to report her to the police. So then why didn't they call the police right then? "I wasn't going to do it," he answered, "because I was giving her the chance to leave on her own and look for work elsewhere. But she wanted revenge."

Although his reasoning seemed coherent and credible, there was a question that needed clarification: Why wasn't this evidence brought up during the trial? According to Quintanilla, it was Valdez, the prosecutor, who didn't want to muddy the case with two different accusations against Yolanda.

Abraham also handed me a copy of a letter that the San Antonio district attorney's office had sent her years ago, before she ever met Selena. In it she was informed that there was a formal inquiry investigating her for committing check fraud. Selena's father discovered the letter when he went through the personal files Yolanda kept in the office at Selena Etc. while searching for evidence to incriminate his daughter's murderer. Although this fraud case had nothing to do with the fan club theft, it was undeniable proof of

Yolanda's lack of honesty according to Abraham. When I called the San Antonio DA's office later, they explained that the case had been closed for a long time because the accused, Yolanda, had agreed to pay back the funds in question. But because the information was confidential, they were not allowed to reveal the exact amount she paid. All they could tell me was that it was more than $750.

The afternoon of our interview, Abraham was certain that Yolanda would soon be charged with having stolen from the fan club. Much to his chagrin, this never happened. Months later, Carlos Valdez announced that for lack of evidence Yolanda would not be charged with fraud. It was a hard blow for Quintanilla, because he had always maintained that it had been the motive behind Yolanda's killing Selena, and now it was a doubtful reason.

Perhaps the most impressive moment of the interview came when Abraham revealed his theory that Yolanda had tried to kill Selena five times before she succeeded. His version was quite detailed and seemed as precise as a detective's.

"There were four attempts to kill her and she killed her on the fifth one. The night of the meeting, Selena talked to her and fired her. The next day, March 10, Selena and Chris went to the bank to take Yolanda's signature off the boutique's account. Now notice that on March 11 Yolanda applied for the gun, when she realized that she really was being fired. On March 13, when they gave her the gun, she went to her lawyer to write up her letter of resignation. In reality, through her resignation she was preparing an alibi … Immediately after seeing her lawyer she went to Corpus and checked into the Sand and Sea Motel in order to kill Selena."

"So what happened? Why didn't she do it?" I asked him.

"It so happened that Selena wasn't in Corpus Christi; she was in Miami. When my daughter arrived the next day," he continued, "Yolanda called her to schedule a meeting with her. Using the excuse that traffic was too heavy to get to Corpus, she asked Selena to meet her at a parking lot— K Bob's parking lot—twenty-five miles from the city! She thought she would kill Selena there. She didn't do it because upon arriving, Selena told her that she could remain in charge of business affairs in Mexico."

According to Abraham, Selena needed Yolanda to follow through with her operations in Monterrey until she was able to find someone to replace her. When they met at K Bob's, in order to avoid problems Selena promised Yolanda that she would not have to deal with her father any longer and that she would just focus on Monterrey. Abraham is convinced that this calmed her down because "she felt that she was still part of our organization." It was then that Yolanda went back to San Antonio and returned the gun.

At that point, Yolanda traveled to Monterrey and Selena to Tennessee to record her new album in English. In Tennessee, Selena realized that several bank documents were missing.

"When Selena realized this," continued Quintanilla, "she called her up and Yolanda panicked. That's why on March 26 she went and got her gun again. And once again she went to a motel and phoned my daughter to try a second assassination attempt."

Abraham says that what saved Selena this time was her fame. When she returned from Tennessee, she went to the motel where her arrival did not go unnoticed. Rumors of her visit spread rapidly among the employees and they came out to ask for her autograph.

"There were too many witnesses and she couldn't kill her there. Look, the pattern's the same as on her first try— when she bought the gun and went to a motel."

Selena and Yolanda had frequent meetings in different motels because Yolanda was living with her parents in San Antonio and she went only to Corpus Christi, which is about two hours away by car, to deal with the singer's business needs. But after being confronted by Abraham, Yolanda was no longer welcome at any of the Quintanilla family's homes or businesses. Selena and she had no other recourse than to meet behind closed doors.

The third attempt—according to Abraham's hypothesis—was planned during her trip to Monterrey on the last week of March. "Ricardo Martínez, a friend of mine from Monterrey, received several calls from Yolanda, who, screaming desperately, told him she had been raped. The following day Yolanda repeated her desperate phone calls, which were always abruptly cut off, as though someone had yanked the phone out of her hand. Martínez sent one of his employees to the hotel where Yolanda was staying and found out that she had left just a few minutes earlier. So all those calls were from the hotel, from her cellular phone. On March 30, she returned to Corpus and called Selena with the same story of the rape … Up until she arrived in Corpus, we heard nothing further from her. All this was a new alibi," Abraham assured me.

When she arrived in Corpus on March 30, she checked into the Days Inn and put her plan into action. Yolanda phoned Selena and asked her to come alone to the motel. What saved her life this third time was that Chris Pérez accompanied her. He waited outside while she spoke with Yolanda and picked up some financial documents.

That same night, after Selena had left, Yolanda called her through her beeper several times. Eventually the singer called back from her house. Yolanda wanted Selena to take her to the hospital. Supposedly she was bleeding due to the rape. "What she was trying to do was to get her to return to the hotel in order to kill her. That was attempt number four," Abraham insisted. But Yolanda did not succeed because Chris did not want his wife to go out again at that late hour. Selena promised to take her to the hospital the following morning.

At first light on March 31, Selena kept her promise. "The rest we know," said Quintanilla as he lowered his gaze. "Selena took her back to the motel and that's where she killed her."

We had gotten to the actual moment when the crime had been committed. According to his theory, it was Abraham who had unmasked Yolanda, who had discovered she was a thief and who had her between a rock and a hard place. The question that followed seemed logical to me: "So why didn't she kill *you* instead of your daughter?"

"She was quite angry at me. What was the most harm she could inflict upon me and my family? Well, by killing

Selena. But if that policeman hadn't stopped her in the motel parking lot, she would have gone on to our offices and shot us all."

"Would you rather she had killed you than your daughter?" I asked, knowing I was touching a very vulnerable spot.

"Yes, I would rather it have been me … she was so young, barely starting her life…" He was not able to continue. Through his dark glasses, I could see tears running down his face. The camera didn't catch it, but I certainly saw him cry.

Selena kept reappearing and it was all too unavoidable and painful. What had her last days been like? Was there something he wished he could have done for his daughter?

"Mr. Quintanilla, a little while ago you brought up the name of Dr. Ricardo Martínez. When we interviewed him, he said he had been someone quite close to Selena in the last days of her life. He was her confidant, doctor, financial adviser, and so on. Now you're saying he was a friend of yours. He told us that Selena had been very sad and alone during the last days of her life."

"The mistake we made was not giving Selena more support in her business," Abraham answered.

"Are you sorrry?" I asked him.

"If I would have given Selena more support in her business affairs … maybe if I had given her more attention, none of this would ever have happened … I was so busy with the music. Without our support, the fox got got into the chicken coop. We left the door open for that woman and look at what she wound up doing!"

For the first time, Abraham publicly admitted having made mistakes. Finally, the hard-edged man we had known all these months showed his human side. Neither he nor those around him were perfect.

"In other words, what Dr. Ricardo Martínez said about her being alone is, in part, because of that?" I asked.

"Yes. We didn't give her the support to fulfill her dream."

Her dream of launching a line of clothing that carried her name ... Was Selena's dream so strong as to make her leave her music behind?

"To say that my daughter was not happy in the world of music is a bunch of crap," he answered. He used almost the same sentiments to respond to the rumors about the relationship between Selena and Chris. "One day before she died, she, my wife and my other daughter, Suzette, went to eat at a restaurant and Selena told them she wanted to have a child. Do you think that indicates that she was unhappy with her husband?"

We took a short break while we changed tapes. Off camera I asked him about something that had always intrigued me: the suitcase full of documents and Selena's clothes that was found in the room at the Days Inn. Abraham maintained that Selena took it so that Yolanda could change since she claimed her clothes were ripped due to the supposed rape. At first, the answer seemed logical and reasonable, but when I tried to envision Yolanda getting into Selena's clothes, weighing fifty more pounds than she did now, it seemed like an impossible task. I could not imagine the woman who was now a convict wearing Selena's favorite jacket, the one inside the suitcase. It was the black leather jacket she used to tape a video with the Barrio Boyzz. Besides, what was the purpose of Selena's permit to work in Mexico that the singer also had with her? It would have been useless to Yolanda. Just as I was getting ready to mention this, we were told that it was time to go on with the interview. Later, off camera again, I tried once more to broach the subject of the suitcase, and Abraham forcefully changed the topic. When he is ready to move on, there is no stopping him. Perhaps he thought his earlier explanation had been sufficient.

I knew the public was curious to know what Abraham thought of the trial and how he had handled his most difficult moments.

"Why do you think Yolanda didn't claim to be temporarily insane in order to get a lesser sentence?" I asked him.

"Because she never regretted doing what she did," he answered. "She never admitted guilt or remorse. If it had been an accident, she would show regret. But that hasn't happened."

"How has all this affected your life from day to day?"

"Well, you can imagine," he answered. "I've never been in a courtroom in my entire life. It leaves quite an impression to be sitting there, having people saying all these things about you as though I were the guilty one: that I was a dictator who controlled my children's lives; that I had raped that woman; and I couldn't defend myself. The first night of the trial, when we went out to eat at a restaurant, I felt that the whole world was staring at me."

As I tried to visualize him looking paranoid, I couldn't help but smile. He smiled, too. I took advantage of that moment to end the interview in the best way possible.

"Well, with the investigation you've shown us, your own, you've almost turned into a detective."

"I'm Columbo," he answered between laughs. "I'm Columbo the detective."

I had never before seen him joke about anything.

11

Tying Up Loose Ends

SUMMER 1996

For better or worse, the trial against Yolanda Saldívar did not solve the mystery behind Selena's death. And without a doubt, my interview with Yolanda only served to magnify the enigma: On top of everything, now there was a secret about the secret! That is why I was not surprised later when allegations and declarations from people close to the singer came out. Just as her father had done during our interview, they wanted to clear up the situation regarding the secret for one reason or another. What you will read here is significant because it sheds light on the complexity of Selena's life. Many of those around her had hidden agendas. But I ask you to look at it the way I do: Keep in mind that there are two sides to every story. Unfortunately, the truth is rarely found in only one of them; it's usually a combination of the two.

Dr. Martínez said all he was about to say a few months after the trial. He spoke openly with a reporter from the American magazine *US*. The article, published in early 1996, did not catch me by surprise at all because before their interview with him, representatives from the magazine called *Primer Impacto* to ask us for help. We gave them copies of the exclusive interview with Yolanda and the one we had with Dr. Martínez. This gave them a foundation for obtaining the impressive revelations from the doctor.

I found one observation made by the journalist who went to see Martínez in Mexico to be quite interesting. She pointed out that before starting to speak, the doctor "turned on the television so that his conversation cannot be heard by his wife, who is sleeping in an adjoining bedroom." Was there a secret the doctor did not want his wife to know? Why would he want to speak behind his wife's back?

The doctor told the reporter, just as he had told us, that there had never been a romance between him and Selena. About his relationship with the singer, he confessed, "When you know a person very well, and you reach a deep understanding [of each other] … This is intimacy, because you can tell everything to this person. You don't have to be their lover." He confessed to details I already knew: He had sent her gifts of floral and fruit arrangements; even when he had not been a fan of Tejano music, he accompanied the singer on promotional trips and had even sat at the table with her during the Tejano Music Awards. On my own I know that he also took her out to dine frequently in Monterrey, which is why it seemed so odd to me that when she died, he did not attend her funeral.

About the Tejano music queen's feelings toward him, Ricardo said, "It may have been possible she loved me, admired me as a man ... and the demonstration of this was in the way she gave me all of her confidence, trusted me with her most intimate things."

According to Martínez, Selena spoke to him several times about how disillusioned she felt with her husband. "Selena was not very happy with her husband ... He had become very small in her eyes because he was not able to act, to make decisions—not as her protector, not as a man."

In the magazine article the doctor verified that Yolanda resented the influence he managed to have over Selena. And for that reason, she tried to undermine it at all costs. Perhaps he was referring to incidents like the one when Selena arrived in Monterrey to find her hotel room full of roses he had sent her—and Yolanda warned her that the doctor wanted to seduce her. Was Yolanda putting ideas in Selena's head because she felt replaced by Martínez? Or as she told me during our interview, was she perhaps trying to protect her friend from a situation that could harm her and to which Selena appeared to be blind? I remember Yolanda's words: "I knew this danger was going to mess things up, that it was going to make her suffer."

As you remember during my interview with Yolanda, she said the role that Martínez played in everything was "part of the secret." She also told me, "He didn't want to talk to my lawyers. Why? Because he was afraid of something.

When he found out that that [particular] thing was not revealed in the trial, [he] relaxed and told you what he told you on TV." This is true. Martínez did not agree to the interview on our show until just after all the evidence had been presented in court and Yolanda was found guilty.

Yolanda assured me that she has Selena's diary in her possession. It is a small book with a lock in which the singer recorded her concerns and joys during a period of two years and where she kept even her most private thoughts as well as songs and poems of love she penned. Selena gave it to Yolanda so she would keep it from falling into the wrong hands. Martínez told the *US* journalist that in his opinion what happened in room 158 had to do with this diary. He believes Selena went to get it back since she no longer trusted in her friend. If he is right, perhaps that is why Selena emptied Yolanda's bag onto the bed minutes before being shot. The singer was desperately searching for the book.

I know the diary is in the Saldívar family's house. I ask myself what Yolanda plans to do with it. She had told me during our interview that when she decides to reveal the supposed secret, she will do so with proof, with documents. Surely the diary is part of that proof. I think if she were to make it public it would be like killing Selena a second time. This time the bullet would lodge in her heart.

Abraham became rabid when the *US* article was published. He condemned the insinuation that Selena might have had an extramarital affair with Dr. Martínez and said that the doctor was and would continue to be a friend of the family. He said that Ricardo was incapable of making statements like the ones published and accused the *US* reporter of being a liar. Fortunately, she had taped her interview with Dr. Martínez in its entirety and was able to stand her ground. I do not know if it is because he found out that the interview was on tape, but the fact is that later, Abraham's attitude toward the doctor changed. Instead of defending him, he stated on a Univisión show that Dr. Martínez was simply a family acquaintance and that any photos of him with Selena existed because she was willing to pose with him, just as she would with any of her fans.

Shortly after the publication of the article about Martínez, Sebastián D'Silva, formerly employed by the doctor, entered the scene. He claims that at one time he was indispensable to the doctor—"his right hand, assistant, bodyguard, friend and confidant." In other words, he was to the doctor everything that Yolanda had been to Selena. It was precisely for that reason that Yolanda and he got along—because among the many things they had in common, they both shared secrets with their respective employers. Many were the times when all four of them went out together.

When Selena died, Sebastián, unlike Martínez, did go to the funeral. He says he drove all the way to Corpus Christi in a car the doctor had lent him. And there are conflicting tales as to why the professional relationship between him and the doctor came to an end shortly after.

I contacted him after reading a detailed interview he gave to the Monterrey newspaper *El Norte*. D'Silva assures in that article that the mysterious ring that slipped from Selena's bloodied hand as she was dying had been a gift from the doctor. He said he accompanied the doctor when he went to purchase it after a medical convention they had attended in New York.

What few people know is that D'Silva was confused. Without knowing it, he was talking about *another* ring, a second one. This piece of jewelry consisted of three intertwining gold circles that formed a band. It was not the same ring that Selena had held in the ambulance. Not long after this, Ernestina Saldívar, one of Yolanda's nieces who had worked in Selena's boutique, spoke with me and made it clear that *both* rings had been gifts from the doctor. Yolanda must have been referring to Dr. Martínez when she told me in the interview that she had only been the go-between in the purchase of the ring with the Fabergé egg design, and that later a third party took care of the bill.

Perhaps before she realized that Dr. Martínez was stealing away her influence over Selena and even when the doctor supposedly represented an imminent danger for her friend, Yolanda had no qualms in acting as a go-between. In fact, D'Silva told *El Norte* that "Yolanda was always good to the doctor. On many occasions he would ask her to call Selena on her cell phone no matter where she might be in the United States and she would do so; she'd put him through. Sometimes Selena would be sleeping and she would call her for him. She performed many favors for him." The same *El Norte* reporter also spoke with Yolanda on one occasion; she told him that Selena's husband had turned to her for advice on how to save his marriage. According to Yolanda, she suggested that Chris take his wife out to have fun; to conquer her again by preparing a romantic meal and not to let her go to Monterrey alone.

Knowing Yolanda, it does not surprise me that she would give him helpful advice—for at one point she loved Chris as a brother. What I do not comprehend is why she was trying to cover all the bases: Why was she trying to help Selena's husband while at the same time working to aid the man she thought had other intentions toward her best friend.

Very few people know the following: Yolanda was convinced that Selena intended to run away with Dr. Martínez, which was why she brought the mysterious suitcase full of clothes and her Mexican work permit to room 158; she argued with Selena in the room because she wanted to stop her, because she wanted to prevent the singer from ruining her own life. Whatever the reasons might be, this scenario was never described in court. When Martínez was questioned about this by a reporter, he responded, "She may have been thinking about it but it was never a reality. But there was a moment in which she wanted to move to Monterrey. Many things are said about this, but not much is certain. You understand this is a very, very, uh, delicate situation. I think Selena understood this, and I think she understood that it would have been impossible."

In his comments in *El Norte,* D'Silva always referred to Yolanda as a victim and said he was positive that Yolanda purchased the revolver because she was receiving threats from Abraham. He claims to have witnessed an incident during which Selena begged Yolanda to return the weapon and not to report her father to the authorities.

His version of events is identical to Yolanda's. It matches up so well that there is no logic to explain why this man was never called to testify in the trial. I finished reading the article and was left wondering: Was Sebastián D'Silva a good person attempting to defend the woman who had been defended solely by her attorney? Was he trying to bring to light a truth that no one was aware of, but one he was deeply familiar with? Or would he turn out to be a greedy stranger looking for an angle?

When I called D'Silva to ask him for a television interview, the first thing he did was to ask for six thousand dollars in exchange for speaking to us. He explained that although he found himself in a precarious financial situation and that his wife had just given birth to a baby girl whom they had named Selena, the money was not for him. It was to pay a lawyer since he feared legal repercussions from Abraham. He acted as if he did not care whether he was interviewed or not, but he spoke as though we needed him. More than once he told me, "I have many things to say, but I cannot speak without getting paid that sum. It's for my protection." According to D'Silva, he and his former boss had agreed on a pact of silence—they would not talk to anyone about Selena. But now that the doctor had broken his promise and had spoken openly, D'Silva felt that he too could do so and in the process he would denounce Abraham for an injustice he had committed against him. It all seemed suspicious to me, but I continued to hear him out. He kept on talking and it was during this part of our conversation that I put certain pieces of the puzzle together and began to suspect that D'Silva was most likely the man whom Selena's father claimed was trying to blackmail him: the very same one whom Abraham had referred to when he called me to agree to our interview. (My suspicions were later confirmed when Quintanilla directly accused D'Silva of blackmail in an article that appeared in a Mexican newspaper.) At the time, Quintanilla's claims had made no sense, but now they did.

As it turns out, D'Silva, acting on the doctor's orders, had always been at Selena's disposal whenever she visited Monterrey. He was responsible for taking Selena and Yolanda wherever they wished and helping them in their dealings to make the clothing factory a reality. He claims that this is how he became a friend to both of them. He says that during the last few months of her life, Selena visited his home several times and, using his telephone, the singer made innumerable long-distance calls.

The Mexican telephone company has confirmed that calls from D'Silva's residence were made to Selena's home and businesses in Texas. Apparently, Selena never paid for them and D'Silva tried to collect for them from Abraham, explaining that as someone with few financial resources, he needed the money to help care for his newborn daughter. Abraham blew up, found the bill to be excessive and told D'Silva to go to hell. The singer's father maintains that D'Silva also tried to charge him a five-thousand-dollar commission for acting as liaison between the Quintanilla family and the owners of a club in Monterrey who had hired Selena to perform two concerts. Abraham admits that D'Silva indeed did introduce him to the nightclub owners, but he says that he personally negotiated his daughter's contract. He feels that all he owes D'Silva is his thanks since "there was no legal financial agreement—spoken or written" between them.

Abraham insists that D'Silva threatened him with revealing intimate details about Selena to the press if he did not get paid. If that is the case, then Martínez's former employee was true to his promise. Not only did he speak to *El Norte*, but he also continued to contact us regarding an interview. I was left with the impression that in reality he wanted the six thousand dollars for himself, not for an attorney.

I never heard from D'Silva again. I only know that his revenge, whether justified or not, achieved certain results. Abraham became quite angry, and even Dr. Martínez showed irritation at Sebastián D'Silva's comments. The doctor only went as far as to say that D'Silva simply had been his chauffeur. Furious and sarcastic at the same time, Abraham told a mutual acquaintance: "Now it seems that everyone in the world swears to have known more about my daughter's life than I do!"

12

The Secret

We return to Selena's secret again. As I told you, Yolanda revealed it to me during our second phone conversation, the day after being found guilty, in her darkest hour. Trapped by desperation, she gave me all her trust. Trust that I respect, confidences for which I am grateful.

For me it became *Yolanda's* secret. I know her version completely and with a great number of details. But she warned me it was off the record, don't forget that. For whatever reason, she wanted to feel in control of the information, to choose the time and place to reveal it. Unfortunately for her, many of the things she told me, but not all of them, became public knowledge bit by bit. Since I knew the story,

I was able to piece the puzzle together and put it in these pages, without breaking my promise. I accepted and still respect her request not to reveal other details she confided to me. For that reason, I shall not mention anything until she changes her mind and presents the evidence to prove her revelations.

The fact is that ever since our earliest conversations, I have been able to confirm several parts of the secret by listening to the words of others. If you have read this far—and if you've read between the lines—you know that I have revealed much in an indirect manner. All the players in this drama have different motivations for holding fast to their stories and saying the things they have said. Some of them are quite noble; others are cool and calculated.

I believe some—but not all—of what Yolanda Saldívar has told me. I will only say that the secret has two parts to it. One part I find hard to believe for lack of evidence; even if Yolanda decides to reveal it, I do not think you would be convinced. The other sounds more logical and is the secret I have tried to explore throughout these pages. The evidence and witnesses presented during the trial confirmed certain details, as did individuals who never took the stand and events that took place far away from the courtroom.

I should say that *nothing* Yolanda told me or that others later revealed was, in my eyes, damaging to Selena's reputation. No person or event indicates that Selena was dishonest or that she had a dark side. To the contrary. I believe she was simply a victim of circumstance.

Selena was a vibrant young woman made of flesh and blood; by the age of twenty-three she had probably made some mistakes—just as I made them at that age, just as you yourself must have made them—but because she lived her life under the watchful eye of the public, her mistakes took on a different meaning.

I was disturbed by the monstrous things that were said after my interview with Yolanda. A range of malicious conclusions were reached: Selena had AIDS; Selena was a drug trafficker. Illogical, irresponsible and stupid comments were made.

I suspect that Yolanda will reveal the secret one day. It's all she has left to keep her in the public eye in order to escape the anonymity of her jail cell. I know at one time she thought of writing a book about her tragedy and that from the beginning she took notes and documented every event in detail. Later she changed her mind.

The secret does not justify the events of March 31. I believe that Yolanda used the secret as a blindfold to avoid seeing the truth. She continues to deny to herself her role in the death of the singer, a defense mechanism, perhaps, that allows her to live with the burden of being a murderer.

If you should see me on the street, ask me whatever you wish, but do not ask me about the secret. It's not only that I can't discuss it; it's also because it's time to give it a rest.

Selena deserves it.

Recent Events

AUTUMN 1996

Once I finished writing this book and its existence became known to the media, there were some predictable reactions. The Quintanillas as well as the Saldívars were completely opposed to the project. Without knowing it, for the first time since Selena's death, the two families agreed on one thing. I respect the comments made by both sides. Everyone has the right to an opinion. I never answered my critics because I stand by my work; I wrote this story without taking sides. I am not the first journalist to write a book about her experiences during an important trial, nor will I be the last one.

When Abraham Quintanilla got wind of the news, late in the summer of 1996, he reverted to his old ways of trying to manipulate the press. He called Univisión to demand that my supervisors stop the publication of this book or else make plans to face the consequences. The executives at Univisión explained to him that this was a personal project of mine in which they could not interfere and that they were confident that anything I wrote would be a serious and professional work. He would not listen and kept on with his threats. Univisión did not back down and gave me their unwavering support. I thank them for their vote of confidence.

Abraham continued with his pressure tactics and forbade that any reporters from *Primer Impacto* be given press passes to enter the studios where the film about his daughter's life was being made. And he went even further: He promised to punish any TV station that supplied *Primer Impacto* any video clips from the making of the movie. For different reasons he also lashed out at the competing network, Telemundo. All in all, he was repeating what he had tried to do during Yolanda's trial. Even now, no one seems to be able to make him understand that the right to freedom of expression through the press is protected by the Constitution and that it should be respected for the benefit of all people. The people have the right to be informed.

As for the Saldívar family, after the interview I stayed in touch with Yolanda through letters. Early in 1996, long before it was public knowledge that I was writing this book, I received a letter from her in which she faulted me for publishing the book. She thought I was going to betray her by revealing what she had told me confidentially. I cannot imagine how she found out about the book project, but I am convinced that even inside her cell she manages to stay well informed, if not better informed than those who walk freely on the street. I wrote her a letter telling her that my project was based on my experiences and investigations on the case. She accepted my explanation because she continued to correspond with me for some time and even invited me to visit her at the penitentiary in Gatesville, Texas, where she is carrying out her sentence. At the time, she was working with her lawyers in preparing the appeal to her case and it seemed a good idea to accept her invitation.

I booked the flights immediately, asked my boss for permission to make the trip and prepared to go see her that same week. I called the prison and spoke to one of the administrators to gain permission to enter. They told me there was no problem, but that the visit could ony take place with authorization from the prisoner. They requested all kinds of personal information for security reasons. When I called them the following day, they informed me to my great surprise that Yolanda had not agreed to the visit. I thought there had been a misunderstanding since she herself had been the one to invite me. I contacted María Elida to tell her what had happened. She spoke with her sister and called me later to tell me why Yolanda had not given her consent: The authorities had not told her that the request for a visit came from me and she had thought wrongly that it was some other journalist. The explanation mystified me. I called the prison again to corroborate her version. The officer in charge of my request assured me that she had spoken personally with Yolanda and had told the prisoner, in great detail, that the request came from me, but that, even so, Yolanda refused. She noticed my surprise and told me, "Yolanda is pulling your leg." I should have known better.

Unbelievably, after that incident Yolanda wrote me once again to ask me to visit her. I ignored the invitation. I got tired of her games and have not written to her since. But I have had news about her through María Elida, who called to tell me that Yolanda was about to drop a bomb of sorts. I became so worked up that I managed to get María Elida to give me advance information on this news. It turned out that Yolanda was getting married. I was shell-shocked. The first question I asked was: To whom? María Elida told me it was a suitor from her past. He had even attended the trial incognito. She told me that she did not know him well and confessed that she was concerned because the man was covered in scars and tattoos. She added that she was happy because Yolanda was happy. During the following days, I kept on asking questions and confessed to María Elida that the situation seemed odd and suspicious. She told me that Yolanda had requested that her fiancé be included on the list of people allowed to visit her in jail. What had happened to me, happened to him—the prison authorities had asked the man for personal information, including his Social Security number, for security reasons. Somehow, María Elida got her hands on the information, and she gave it to me for an exclusive in exchange for my letting her know if there was anything unusual about his personal background. I immediately called on my friend the detective and asked him to do a background check. When he called me a short while later, his first words were "Who is that guy? Why do you want this information?" It turned out that Yolanda's future husband was a professional criminal with a mile-long record. He had been in prison in several states for different crimes from assault and robbery to murder. My friend, who was used to dealing with the worst sort when it came to criminals, said to me, "This one's really a winner."

María Elida thanked me for the report. The wedding, needless to say, was canceled. I never found out if Yolanda knew her would-be husband's history beforehand and, as I told you, I have not spoken to her since. I stayed in touch with María Elida a bit longer until one day I read a newspaper article in which she denounced my book. She personally felt offended and surprised by the news, since she had not been aware of my plans. She was resentful that I might be trying to profit financially by using her sister. The truth is that she knew about the project from the very beginning and many were the times when I phoned her with the explicit purpose of asking her questions whose answers would be part of my research for the book. I do not know why she said what she did. I stopped calling her—not because I thought less of her, but out of respect. If she truly felt that way, there was no reason to ask her to justify herself or make her feel uncomfortable.

This book has reached your hands despite everything and everyone. I always dreamed of writing a book, but I never thought I would find myself writing about real people and real events. If I do this again, I'll write fiction, where I can invent the characters and make them good or bad and change the course of history. In real life, destiny is destiny. No author's pen could have changed the inescapable destiny of Selena.